Pathfinder 33

# Stimulating grammatical awareness:
# a fresh look at language acquisition

# The Pathfinder Series

## Active learning — listening and reading

**Reading for pleasure in a foreign language** (PF2)
*Ann Swarbrick*                          ISBN 0 948003 98 7

**Developing skills for independent reading** (PF22)
*Iain Mitchell & Ann Swarbrick*          ISBN 1 874016 34 8

**Creative use of texts** (PF21)
*Bernard Kavanagh & Lynne Upton*         ISBN 1 874016 28 3

**Listening in a foreign language** (PF26)
A skill we take for granted?
*Karen Turner*                           ISBN 1 874016 44 5

## Supporting learners and learning

**Teaching learners how to learn**
Strategy training in the ML classroom (PF31)
*Vee Harris*                             ISBN 1 874016 83 6

**Making effective use of the dictionary** (PF28)
*Gwen Berwick and Phil Horsfall*         ISBN 1 874016 60 7

**Nightshift** (PF20)
Ideas and strategies for homework
*David Buckland & Mike Short*            ISBN 1 874016 19 4

**Grammar matters** (PF17)
*Susan Halliwell*                        ISBN 1 874016 12 7

## Planning and organising teaching

**Assessment and planning in the MFL department** (PF29)
*Harmer Parr*                            ISBN 1 874016 71 2

**Departmental planning and schemes of work** (PF11)
*Clive Hurren*                           ISBN 1 874016 10 0

**Fair enough?** (PF14)
Equal opportunities and modern languages
*Vee Harris*                             ISBN 1 874016 03 8

**Foreign Language Assistants** (PF32)
A guide to good practice
*David Rowles, Marian Carty
and Anneli McLachlan*                    ISBN 1 874016 95 X

**Bridging the gap** (PF7)
GCSE to 'A' level
*John Thorogood & Lid King*              ISBN 0 948003 89 8

**Improve your image** (PF15)
The effective use of the OHP
*Daniel Tierney & Fay Humphreys*         ISBN 1 874016 04 6

## Teaching/learning in the target language

**On target** (PF5)
Teaching in the target language
*Susan Halliwell & Barry Jones*          ISBN 0 948003 54 5

**Keeping on target** (PF23)
*Bernardette Holmes*                     ISBN 1 874016 35 5

## Motivating all learners

**Yes — but will they behave?** (PF4)
Managing the interactive classroom
*Susan Halliwell*                        ISBN 0 948003 44 8

**Not bothered?** (PF16)
Motivating reluctant language learners in Key Stage 4
*Jenifer Alison*                         ISBN 1 874016 06 2

**Communication re-activated** (PF6)
Teaching pupils with learning difficulties
*Bernardette Holmes*                     ISBN 0 948003 59 6

**Differentiation** (PF18)
Taking the initiative
*Anne Convery & Do Coyle*                ISBN 1 874016 18 6

## Cultural awareness

**Crossing frontiers** (PF30)
The school study visit abroad
*David Snow & Michael Byram*             ISBN 1 874016 84 4

**Languages home and away** (PF9)
*Alison Taylor*                          ISBN 0 948003 84 7

**Exploring otherness** (PF24)
An approach to cultural awareness
*Barry Jones*                            ISBN 1 874016 42 9

## Broadening the learning experience

**New contexts for modern language learning** (PF27)
Cross-curricular approaches
*Kim Brown & Margot Brown*               ISBN 1 874016 50 X

**With a song in my scheme of work** (PF25)
*Steven Fawkes*                          ISBN 1 874016 45 3

**Drama in the languages classroom** (PF19)
*Judith Hamilton & Anne McLeod*          ISBN 1 874016 07 0

**Being Creative** (PF10)
*Barry Jones*                            ISBN 0 948003 99 5

All Pathfinders are available through good book suppliers or direct from **Grantham Book Services**,
Isaac Newton Way, Alma Park Industrial Estate, Grantham, Lincs NG31 9SD.
Fax orders to: 01476 541 061. Credit card orders: 01476 541 080

**Pathfinder 33**

A CILT series for language teachers

# Stimulating grammatical awareness

## A fresh look at language acquisition

*Heather Rendall*

Centre for Information
on Language Teaching and Research

*The views expressed in this publication are the author's and do not necessarily represent those of CILT.*

First published 1998
Copyright © 1998 Centre for Information on Language Teaching and Research
ISBN 1 902031 08 3

A catalogue record for this book is available from the British Library
Printed in Great Britain by Oakdale Printing Co Ltd

Published by the Centre for Information on Language Teaching and Research,
20 Bedfordbury, Covent Garden, London WC2N 4LB

CILT Publications are available from: Grantham Book Services, Isaac Newton Way, Alma Park Industrial Estate, Grantham, Lincs NG31 8SD. Tel: 01476 541 080. Fax: 01476 541 061. Book trade representation (UK and Ireland): Broadcast Book Services, 24 De Montfort Road, London SW16 1LZ. Tel: 0181 677 5129.

# Contents

# Introduction

In 1989 the Government introduced a 'Languages for All' policy into schools. As a result many teachers of Modern Foreign Languages were faced with a situation, which to them was both novel and challenging - namely teaching across the whole ability range. They may have welcomed the move and greeted the policy with open arms, but it was something for which, however many years' teaching experience they may have already had, many of them were not prepared.

Methodologies that had been honed to a fine art no longer worked: knowledge and understanding that previously, when dealing with a selected top 20% of the ability range could be taken for granted, could no longer be counted on. Mistakes and misunderstandings never before encountered became stock-in-trade of many daily lessons.

While pressures have increased yearly to raise the number of pupils gaining, first, a GCSE and now a 'good' GCSE, teachers have despaired of the seemingly never-ending list of skills and competencies that were being added to the list of 'Things to Cover'. Time constraints have been added to the pressure and often as result content has been pursued at the cost of a thorough grounding: topics have led the way and comprehension and competence have lagged behind.

This book takes a lateral look at learning. Rather than start with conventional methodology and attempt to stretch it across the ability range, it looks at the learner and asks:

- 'Why is it that some of them cannot just use and apply what we teach them?'
- 'Why do they make the mistakes they do?'
- 'Do their misunderstandings and errors tell us anything about how they approach language learning and what is going on in their minds?'
- 'Can we fathom what they are making of what we are teaching?'
- 'Are there gaps that we haven't seen?'
- Are there needs that we are not addressing?'

Using actual examples of pupil error, an attempt is made to answer these questions and then to suggest practical ideas for classroom use.

# Handy references to activities

Numbers in brackets refer to pages.

CILT

# 1.    Doing what comes naturally

It's a funny thing — language learning. We all seem to do it so easily first time around — so much so that there is a school of thought among linguists who believe that by researching into a child's acquisition of its mother tongue and applying those 'natural' methods to foreign language learning, they will arrive at some linguistic Philosopher's Stone — a method that will be successful with all.

And yet the reality of most foreign language learning is anything but natural. By force of circumstances it is restricted for most people to a school-based experience. Contact time is often a mere two hours a week. There is little or no support in the surrounding environment. Only a minority of pupils or students have families who can offer help and guidance up to exam level and beyond. And there is no real pressure or motivation, in this country at least, that drives pupils to learn and then make use of any language once it is learnt.

But even if we could change these negative factors into the most positive set of circumstances possible, there are still two important differences between the natural language learning of a baby/child and the school-based language learning of a child/pupil.

## THE NEED FOR A MEANS OF COMMUNICATION

A baby, from birth, communicates using cries and screams or smiles and gurgles. But these are not enough; the child is encouraged ceaselessly by the humans that surround it, to develop and take part in the method of communication called language. It gradually becomes a two way process that, as it evolves, inter alia makes sense of the infant's surroundings and the events that take place. It is also crucial to the initial process of building up inner thought and all those cognitive procedures that will one day produce reason and judgement, fear and superstition, humour and wit and all those other characteristics of the human mind.

By contrast, at ten or eleven years of age, which is when the great majority of pupils first learn a foreign language, all this is already in place. Pupils have a common means of verbal communication with their teacher and their fellow pupils, which is, in the majority of cases, their mother tongue. They have a finely developed process of inner thought and are able to understand and make sense of the world around them more or less successfully. The driving forces that power the need for developing a system of communication are absent.

## RECOGNISING WORDS

To a baby, language is pure sound. Using a method still not clearly understood, over the first few years of its existence, it is ever more able to differentiate the various and varying elements of sound chains, identify them with increasing sophistication with meaning and apply and reapply them both in listening and then speaking.

To a ten- or eleven-year-old, language is more than sound. It is words. During six years of primary education, the emphasis within the curriculum has been on reading and writing. Language has been changed from a pure state to one of artificiality. Instead of just saying what you think and understanding what you hear, knowing a language system now means being able to write down what you think or have heard and understand and report back what you have read, Primary education has turned pupils into literate beings; they are capable of turning sound into words and words into sound.

So even if we could provide the best of environments for learning a second language — constant contact with the language, motivation for its use, support and encouragement from those around — we still would not have the same natural state of mind in our pupils as a baby has. There is no guarantee that 'natural' methods of learning would now be the best way to learn.

Rather than look at what the language learning of babes and infants might tell us about language learning in general, it may prove more fruitful then if, instead, we look at the natural tendencies of first-time second or foreign language learners. During the initial learning period, do learners of second or foreign languages exhibit any distinctive behaviours? Can we predict their actions and reactions? Can we identify areas of possible confusion and error and act to minimise them? In brief, is there such a thing as 'natural language learning' a second time around?

Obviously any conclusions drawn here will not be universal. A pupil with good memorisation skills will always outperform a fellow pupil with poor learning skills. A pupil who has extensive experience of another country, another culture, another language, has the advantage over the monolingual person from a narrow background. Pupils who have the confidence to use new language, will go further than those who put in little effort.

That having been said, it may still be possible to delineate situations that are common to average pupils beginning their first foreign language lessons and list possible reactions and expected responses; we just have to bear in mind, when considering our own pupils, that these statements may fit more or less well and their progress through them may be more or less fast and thorough.

## MAKING SENSE OF A NEW LANGUAGE

To the average monolingual, any new language is pure babble. No sense can be made of the sounds at all. In fact, the sounds appear as a continuous stream of noise; the pauses and word/phrase breaks are not discernible. It all seems very fast indeed and serves only to reaffirm the worst suspicions of many that here is something far beyond their grasp — they are never going to be able to understand, let alone speak another language.

The one skill that rescues our pupils is imitation; children are far better at imitating than adults. They can repeat longer phrases; they can reproduce exact intonation; they can produce between two and six phrases or short sentences held in their heads in short-term memory, even when they don't fully understand the meaning of what they are saying. And they find it fun — mostly! So the first series of foreign language lessons usually offers the opportunity to repeat after the teacher a set number of phrases or short sentences, usually answers to simple questions referring to personal details such as name, age, address and family. All of this is well within the capability of most pupils and both we and they are pleased (and proud) of the apparent progress being made.

But we should not mistake accurate imitation for progress and understanding. Wholesale copying, both in speaking and in writing, is possible where the general meaning is understood, but the actual value of the individual elements of the language itself can be entirely misunderstood.

How else can errors such as '*je m'appelle grand*' be accounted for? Obviously, the pupil wished to say 'I am big'. She delved into her store of language learnt and experienced — in this case — over two terms in Year 7 and retrieved the phrase '*je m'appelle*' for the meaning of 'I am', such as in the sentence 'I am Sarah' = '*Je m'appelle Sarah*'.

The pupil would be capable of making a correct reply both orally and in writing to the question '*Comment t'appelles-tu?*' and so there would be no evidence of poor learning or misconception. And yet, however, the question had been understood 'What's your name?' or 'What are you called?' or 'Who are you?', the reply was clearly understood to say 'I'm Sarah'. And the elements of the sentence therefore had to parallel each other in the following manner: 'I'm' & 'Sarah' = '*Je m'appelle*' & '*Sarah*'.

- Have you noticed any such misunderstandings from your pupils? They are more frequently observed in the early stages of learning, but similar misunderstandings can appear for the first time at any stage.
- Do you teach phrases globally?
- Or do you explain each element in the new language to your pupils?

## 'CHUNKS' LEARNING

Many teachers will recognise a phase that a large number of pupils go through when, having learnt new vocabulary, they tend to overapply it.

For example: having successfully learnt and practised sentences with '*j'aime*', when they move onto other persons' likes and dislikes, they re-use the whole sound as if it constituted the single invariable concept — 'like'.

> '*j'aime*' >> '*papa j'aime*' or even >> '*papa jem*'

Or if a verb has been learnt initially from the infinitive, then it is that form that is used to express all manner of meanings :

> *je aller*     *mes amis aller*     *je suis aller*

It is as if the initial sound and meaning have become a single invariable concept, which is so fixed in the mind that the pupils find it hard to move onto the next stage of adapting or changing the word according to any grammatical demands.

- Is this a very common habit across the ability range?
- Or is it more prevalent among a certain range of pupils?
- If you have recognised it, when would you first expect to see it in the work of your pupils? Very soon? After a term or two? In the second year?
- How long does it take for a pupil to 'get through' this stage?
- Do all pupils successfully 'get through'?

## HOME-MADE PHONETICS

The example given above, '*papa jem*', is evidence of yet another phase to be seen during the initial stages of learning. Words are written phonetically, that is according to mother tongue phonetics — and home-made phonetics at that.

An analysis of error in free production of writing reveals a large percentage of misspellings that fall into this category. In Year 7 the number will be high; and the less able the pupil, the greater the percentage. Among common examples to be seen are

'*je mappel*' '*jabbite*' '*Ya*' '*Nine*'

Some Year 11 pupils are still producing written work along these lines: other pupils seem to be able to avoid doing it from day one.

- What does this evidence tell us about the ways in which pupils are storing and retrieving vocabulary?
- What conclusions can we draw about pupils who show evidence of this kind of home-grown phonetic writing?
- What conclusions can we draw about pupils who show no evidence of it?
- What can we do about it?

These are just a few examples of pupil production that you may have encountered. What they reveal are, on the whole, predictable patterns of behaviour, whose origins can be traced. Once the cause is understood, steps can be taken to either minimise their influence or redress the imbalance of comprehension. It is also possible to accelerate pupils past these areas of difficulty by introducing new and necessary patterns of thought or procedures for storage and retrieval and then constantly and consistently practising them until these patterns and procedures become automatic; that is until they become cognitive skills.

The theories being put forward here have been drawn up as a result of classroom observations over a number of years, analyses of pupils' work and discussions with pupils. They are based on the chaos theory of physics which states that at first everything is chaos! Through random interactions, stable forms emerge. Through trial and error, patterns are established.

Depending on prior experience and knowledge which could be on a sliding scale from nothing to something, our pupils' initial understanding and reaction to a foreign language will be one of linguistic chaos. They can make no sense of what they see or hear. They rely on natural skills of imitation and mimicry, but these skills have limitations. When it comes to understanding the individual elements that go to make up the language, then like all second and foreign language learners everywhere, pupils will make use of their existing language skills.

> *The learner's knowledge of L1 . . . forms a basic resource to which the learner, in the initial stages of learning, can turn in his making use of general language principles.*

> (Ringbom, 1988)

Unfortunately, this does not always produce successful strategies. If what is being taught in the foreign language has no counterpart in the mother tongue, then by turning to their knowledge of their own language, pupils are not going to be helped along useful or even correct lines.

## FALSE HYPOTHESES

When Patricia Manning wanted to discover by what method or reasoning her Year 7 and Year 9 pupils allocated gender to French nouns, she set them a test and then interviewed them about how they had tackled the task. Had they made a point of learning the gender of nouns? Had they developed a feel for masculine or feminine words? Had they taught themselves some successful rules-of-thumb?

What she uncovered was disturbing. Yes, they had taught themselves some rules-of-thumb. Unfortunately they were not successful ones — but they were what the pupils had worked out for themselves and so the pupils persisted in using them. Among the reasons they gave for allocating gender were:

> *words containing many* e*'s or ending in* e *were . . . masculine (!);*

> *words for big, powerful, strong and mobile things were masculine;*
> *words for small, soft, static things were feminine;*

> *words with lots of vowels were feminine;*
> *words with lots of consonants were masculine;*

> *strong sounding words were masculine;*
> *soft sounding words were feminine;*

and perhaps most disturbing of all (for teachers at least)

> *. . . for words for which one couldn't decide, one used* l'

> (Manning, 1991)

Manning's conclusions were that pupils needed to have their attention brought very explicitly to the importance of learning the correct gender and applying the correct form of articles and resolved to include much more of this in her work with all ages and abilities. Her research also shows us just how important it is that some time should be spent in discussion with pupils in order to discover what strategies and hypotheses about the language they have developed and whether or not they are an aid or a hinderance.

## CHOOSING WHAT SUITS YOUR SITUATION BEST

The following chapters will look at some of the most important areas of linguistic chaos that an average eleven-year-old beginning a first foreign language may experience. Ways will be suggested in which teachers can stimulate and encourage the development of vital initial learning skills.

Not everything that follows may apply to the pupils you teach. Like other methodologies, they will be more or less applicable depending on the abilities and learning skills your pupils bring with them into the classroom.

So, for example, if your pupils have been brought up in their primary education to learn yards of poetry off by heart, then they will be more capable of learning-homeworks, i.e. learning words and phrases off by heart, than pupils who have never been asked to learn anything off by heart in their lives. The former will know how to set about it; they will know that they can do it — with a bit of hard work; they will know what it takes and how long it takes.

The latter won't have a clue. They won't know where to start; they may be convinced that this is beyond them; they may not realise how long they have to keep at it. Convinced of their own inadequacies, they may give up far too soon and so unfortunately confirm their own worst fears.

It may help if, while reading, you keep the image of a bar chart in mind — a chart that represents 100% of your pupils in any one Year.

| 0% | 100% |
|---|---|

Then, as you decide whether or not any particular idea would be useful to you, you can be mentally building up a series of bars that relate directly to your pupils across a particular Year.

For example: How much time should be spent on teaching accurate learning?

This will depend on existing learning and spelling skills.

It will depend on the percentage of your pupils in Year 7 who have good spelling skills, before they start their foreign language learning

It will differ between schools.

Here are three different examples:

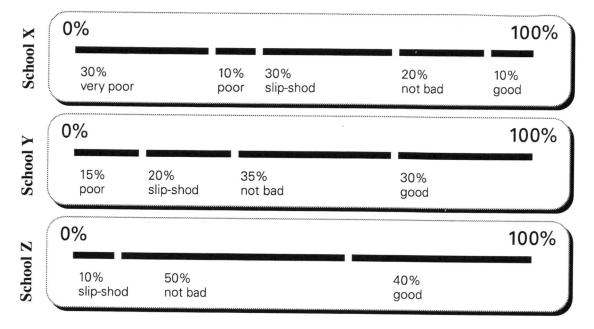

Obviously, School X should be spending more time on developing and ensuring accurate learning skills than School Y or Z. Even School Z, though, needs to make sure that the bottom 10% are helped to improve and are not just written off as poorer learners.

It is not being suggested that all the pupil behaviours described here will be seen in all schools and classes. Some of the situations you may recognise only too well. Others you may never have come across. They are, however, all genuine examples. In reading through the following chapters, you will have to be constantly comparing what is being described to your own situation. If the evidence of your own experience is mirrored in any of the examples, then the suggestions given may be of some help.

Some of the statements made, some of the conclusions drawn contradict current practice and methodological theory. Again, you will have to decide for yourself which theory or theories the evidence of your own experience supports.

# 2. The seeing ear

Of all the four language skills — reading, writing, listening and speaking — listening is first and foremost. It is possible to learn a language — even a first language — with this skill alone: children unable to verbalise because of physical impairment are still able to learn, understand and respond to language. So listening is the first focus of our attention.

As has already been pointed out in the previous chapter, our Year 7 pupils do not just have natural listening skills. They have been educated to 'see' what they hear; to understand that all sound can be translated into words. They are, in this sense, literate. The speed at which we follow speech and make sense of it, under natural circumstances, using our mother tongue, is miraculously fast. We do not need to consciously see the words in our mind's eye. But we can hear where they are, we can separate them and their meanings in order to make sense of what we hear and we can do this so well that, if need be, we can write down what we hear — more or less accurately. None of these skills is immediately available to the learner of a foreign language. They have to be relearnt.

One of the major battle grounds of primary education in any mother tongue is the development of accurate orthography : a battle fought against accepted spelling and 'heard' words. An English child who writes 'receeved', 'gimme', 'wassat' or 'hospittle' is not retrieving spellings that have been seen: rather they are his or her own creation. Had the words or phrases been spoken rather than written, no inaccuracy would have been noticeable, as the primitive phonics succeed in reproducing more or less the correct sound. It is only in written work that the homespun phonetics will be apparent and will be marked down as misspellings,

What causes a child to misspell, that is to store and retrieve according to its own phonetics? Two possible situations:

**1** The child does not have sight of the correct spelling often enough.

**2** When errors do become apparent, they are tolerated and not drawn to his or her attention, so no corrections are ever made.

**But what can also be deduced from such evidence is that a child can and does store sounds that he or she hears and, if the correct spelling is unknown, retrieves them for writing using an individually devised spelling system.** The system so created may be obvious and therefore interpretable by all, e.g. 'Wright a senten to a penfirend' or it can be so individual as to defy outside interpretation, e.g. 'I no binna colla savage'.

ci**LT**

A Year 7 pupil, hearing a foreign language for the first time, is likely to employ this same skill to make sense of the stream of sound being experienced, but cannot as yet separate it into individual words and phrases. If asked to reproduce either orally or in writing any of the sounds, the pupil will have to retrieve them from memory. However they have been stored, the child will decode what has been stored using the phonic system he or she is used to. This could be correct English phonics or it could be an individual system. In speaking, except for the probable heavy accent, the recall should produce a correct response. In writing however we can expect such spellings as:

*Wee*   *J'mapple*   *Shebeet*   *Jai abet*   *saprairde*   *j'e noe na pai*

Mistakes like this are evidence that our pupils are storing by sound, which they then interpret into written form using their own homespun phonetics. The reasons for doing this will be similar to those given for the mother tongue. Not enough sight of the words themselves and not enough correction to change the stored image or interpretation of sound.

How do we avoid this? The answer would be obvious, were it not for a fear of contravening current thinking, which advocates the introduction of new vocabulary by sound and meaning alone, without sight of the word.

In the MFL proposals *Modern Foreign Languages for ages 11 to 16* it states:

> *In the early stages of learning, the written form of a foreign language can interfere strongly with pronunciation, especially where the script is already familar. To combat this, learners need ample opportunities to listen and respond before the written forms are involved.*
>
> *Modern Foreign Languages for ages 11 to 16: 55, 9.6*

Within the last twelve months a newly qualified teacher has told me that during her PGCE she had been taught that all vocabulary should be introduced orally and that the written form should not be introduced until two weeks later. When I asked why, she could give no reason. She had not queried what she had been taught. She had just accepted it and put it into practice.

Another NQT, who had been taught similarly, suggested to me on another occasion that it is a more 'natural' methodology because babies manage to learn words by listening only; they can't read. This had been her own deduction; she too had been given no theoretical background to support the methodology.

Although I can sympathise with the argument about pronunciation, I cannot agree with the conclusion that the solution should be to withdraw the sight of the word. Rather than cure one problem, I believe it may cause another even greater one.

If pupils are being asked to store sound without having ever seen the phonic system by which it is conventionally written, i.e. its correct target language form, then it should come as no surprise to us that they will store it according to their own or their mother-tongue system. Although this may work well — seemingly — while only oral work is required, errors in storage will become apparent as soon as the words are written down.

If words or phrases are inaccurately stored, there is no chance at all of them being retrieved accurately. Even worse, there is some evidence to show that language stored inaccurately early on is only re-learnt correctly with a great deal of effort on behalf of both pupil and teacher. Without that effort, the original storage/retrieval fossilises. Year 11 pupils will have had plenty of opportunity over five years to have corrected for themselves or to have had corrected by their teachers that most basic of responses: '*Je m'appelle . . .*' but '*je mapple*' still occurs and so do half a dozen other alternative spellings.

In order to be able to recognise a sound and associate it with meaning in one's mind, a system of recall has to be built up. Some people depend more on aural recall than visual graphemic recall: that is they recall by hearing the words inside their head rather than seeing the words spelt out . Some people are entirely graphemic: they see words clearly printed in their mind's eye. Others use a mixture of both. In order that all pupils should have the opportunity to build up their own personal recall systems, they need the stimulus of both the sound and the sight of the word. So the very first suggestion is:

The aim is to develop in the pupils the ability to 'see' words heard.

> **!** *A*lways introduce vocabulary using the sound AND the written word.

- First they have to be able to match sound and meaning to the written word.
- Then they must be able to pick out the correct written equivalent when they hear the word or phrase spoken.
- Then they have to be able to visualise the word when they hear it.
- They have to be able to distinguish between correct and incorrect versions of the word or phrase.
- And then finally they have to be able to produce the correct version both orally and in writing, checking all the time with the internalised version now carried inside their head.
- When they can do all of this, they will have learnt the word.

## CONNECTING SIGHT TO SOUND AND MEANING

When introducing new words in class, show the words on separate flashcard labels; these can then be used to play games with the new words.

### MATCHING LABELS TO PICTURES

Divide the class into three or four teams: give each a set of pictures/flashcards and word labels and allocate a 'home wall'. The team to pin up correctly labelled the new vocabulary on its wall is the winner. While they are sorting out the pictures and labels, keep calling out the words in the target language.

C*i*LT

## MATCHING LABELS TO SOUND

Use the same labels for a more sedentary exercise: hand out a label to each pupil. As you say the word or phrase and hold up the flashcard picture, the pupil or pupils holding that label have to hold it up. You can gradually couch words and phrases to be learnt in ever more language so that the ear is being trained to listen out for and recognise certain specific sounds for which the pupil has a written prompt. You can also, as vocabulary increases, hand out more than one label to be listened for.

## LISTENING OUT FOR YOUR WORD

No labels this time. Create a short story in which the word/phrases being learnt appear and re-appear. Ask pupils to listen. When they hear the word or phrase that was on their label in the other exercises, they have to stand up. When they hear it a second time, they sit down. A third time and they stand up again and so on. Once the story has been read through once, read it through again and again, only faster!

**EXTRA**   In low ability classes instead of handing out a list of words to learn to the whole class, make each child responsible for learning one word or phrase on behalf of the class. That child then becomes the 'class expert' on that word — its meaning , its sound and its spelling, its gender. Pupils should be encouraged to refer to the 'class experts' for help — unless of course they find that they have remembered other people's words as well as their own.

## PRACTICE FOR THE EARS AND EYES

From recognising one word labels, move on to devise exercises where the task is:

* to pick out and number words in the order heard.
* to pick words out from a selection of similar looking words or phrases
* to be able to locate words and phrases in texts.

This should prepare them well for being able to locate what you say on a page in the textbook.

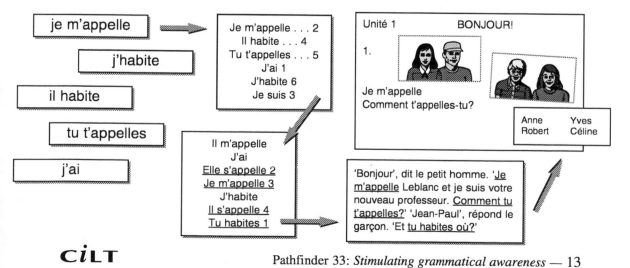

Exercises like these should always precede the type of oral/aural repetition work which is more usual in the first few lessons of any new topic. If we do not 'fix' the sound of new words in our pupils' brains before we ask them to say them, then all we can expect is immediate imitation. This is transitory. They will have difficulty in producing the same sound a few minutes later by themselves and will have to rely on our prompting them.

### SAYING WHAT WE SEE

*I*mitation and repetition are important learning tools. They should not be confused with speaking.

In order to build up correct recall systems, pupils need lots of imitation and repetition exercises and games. These help fix the sound in the brain. Whatever the exercise or game, the sound should be supported by the written word. This will help pupils develop a 'feel' for target language phonics and its spelling by associating from the start the look of the word with the sound.

*G*ive pupils specific time and opportunity to say the words to themselves.

It is also important that pupils should be encouraged to imitate and repeat silently, i.e. to sub-vocalise the sound of new words. This is an important step towards internal recall and later on to thinking, and yet few exercises ever ask this of pupils. When I have suggested it, some pupils have appeared suprised, even shocked, that they should be asked to 'think' in the target language!

A pupil cannot produce the sound of a word independently, unless that sound is well and truly lodged in its head. Once pupils can 'hear' the word inside their heads, they will try and say it. Even then they might have difficulty in actual forming the sounds. Some pupils are quite happy to 'have a go'. They don't mind being corrected and will repeat words happily to themselves until they get it right. Others are not so self-assured. They prefer to wait until they feel more certain about being able to say the word correctly. Known as the 'Silent Period', it is an important step even in first language learning. It is as if the brain needed time to sort out the sound for itself before production. So we should not be insisting that all children speak/imitate simultaneously and immediately. Rather allow imitation and repetition to be voluntary, as they feel confident.

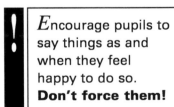

*E*ncourage pupils to say things as and when they feel happy to do so. **Don't force them!**

This is the 'Golden Rule' in the Primary Immersion Scheme in Canada. The teachers use French all the time, but Year 1 pupils are allowed to use whichever language they like. As their understanding and competence grows, so does their confidence and they move almost unconsciously into the target language.

Some pupils will rush at imitation and repetition. Others will wait on the sidelines. Both attitudes should be tolerated. How many slow starters in first language learning catch up with their prattling peers? A silent child can suddenly burst out into sentences. What is certain is that when a child can do something, it will. If it doesn't feel sure about it, it will hesitate and keep silent. Forcing performance may only serve to discourage.

CiLT

## WHEN THE EASY BECOMES HARD

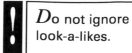

**!** *D*o not ignore look-a-likes.

Many European languages contain a large percentage of words that appear to make learning easy — because they look exactly like or very similar to an English word and very often have the same or similar meaning.

Far from making learning easy, look-a-likes can cause problems throughout language learning careers, but especially at the beginning.

At the very moment when a teacher is trying to develop in the pupils firstly a recognition of a different phonic system and then its use, it is crucial that due emphasis is given to words that are instantly recognised and understood. If they are taken for granted, then they will be taken as read . . . in English. For example: of the first names listed on p13, two appear to pose no problem — Anne and Robert. In fact it is only in the written form they are instantly recognisable. In the spoken form they are not at all as easy to discern. Many textbooks introduce a foreign language using personal details including names and addresses, and yet names of both people and places are notoriously difficult to understand and recognise. Turn this to your advantage: rework them and use them as listen/recognising/ pinpointing exercises.

It is not just names. A pupil seeing the word '*le garage*' or '*la table*' for the first time does not need to be told what they mean. But hearing them for the first time is a totally different matter. Because they are so obvious to us, we should not take it for granted that the same connection is being made by our pupils. If we do not emphasise the difference in sound, we again cannot be suprised if for ever and a day our pupils pronounce them *à l' anglaise* . . . and at the same time have great difficulty in recognising them when heard.

Barreau

Deschamps

Martin

Guérin

Georges

Roulet

Blandin

Desailly

Stefan

Paul

Oliver

Barbara

Claudia

Anna

Michael

Joseph

This is particularly true of French, where a glance at vocabulary introduced over the first term will reveal a high percentage of look-a-likes. Using their **English** reading skills, pupils will recognise these words when met for the first time and unless we take pains to tie these existing skills to new sounds, then when the word is needed, it will be recalled via the English system — no new target language system having been created for it.

Here lies the most probable cause of the problem quoted above about the influence of the written word on pronunciation. **English pronunciation will rule — if we do not insist on replacing it or adding to it the elements of the target language system for pronunciation.**

Over 25% of errors expected in the GCSE oral exam which are graded as zero, are English pronunciation of look-a-like words:

*famille/Familie    camping/Campingplatz    Hôtel    sandwich,* etc

Which means that we have evidence yet again that bad habits learnt early on become engrained over five years of language learning and are hard to eradicate.

So a deliberate effort must be made from the start to distinguish between English and target language sounds for similar looking words. Exercises should be carried out consistently over the five years of language learning. Even if the pupils' attention is not drawn explicitly to the point in question, they will have had the chance to develop for themselves awareness of one of the most important insights into foreign language learning:

It is an easy matter to make sure that in any vocabulary learning, what look like obvious words are included. '*La table*' still needs its gender and its pronunciation learnt, even if its meaning is clear.

> *I*f it looks like English, the last thing it is going to do is sound like English.

| When giving out vocabulary to be learnt, a long list can be reduced to manageable proportions by sorting the words into three groups: | If testing vocabulary discretely, you can make use of these three categories. |
|---|---|
| **1** Those that are instantly recognisable and have the same meaning . These must be learnt for gender and pronunciation. | **1** You say these words in the target language and the pupils write down the English meaning, i.e. can they recognise the TL sound? |
| **2** Those that look like the English or nearly like English and have a different meaning. These are traps! Watch out for them and make sure you know the meaning. | **2** These you either ask for the TL word having given the non-alike meaning, or you say the word in the TL and ask for the English. |
| **3** Those that look like nothing you know and everything has to be learnt. | **3** These you ask for the TL word in the conventional manner. |

## PRACTICE MAKES PERFECT

Some topics will throw up more look-a-like vocabulary than others. This does not make the topic any easier. It just means that the emphasis on learning is different.

For example:

In a topic such as school subjects where the vocabulary is so near to our own, matching meaning visually, i.e. reading the words and understanding them, comes easily. So we should be compensating by spending time practising recognition by sound and committing the correct spelling to memory.

## LISTEN AND ORDER EXERCISES

The 'listen and order' exercises recommended earlier are a good way of dealing with look-a-likes.

> Mathe
> Deutsch
> Englisch
> Kunst
> Religion
> Musik
> Sport
> Informatik

- Print out a list of vocabulary on small pieces of paper — one for each pupil. You can produce twelve lists like this on one sheet of A4.
- At the beginning of the lesson, hand out one list to each pupil and then call out one word at a time, marking down the order in which you say them.
- Pupils have to number the words in the order they hear them — in this instance 1–8.
- At the end choose a pupil to be a checker, to read the words aloud in the order given.
- Repeat the whole exercise two or three times, reordering the words each time.
- Whenever there is a natural break in the lesson, inbetween exercises, ask the pupils to pick up the lists again and read the words aloud again, always using a different order.
- Once it is clear pupils are becoming adept, appoint a pupil to read the list aloud.
- If, as in the example given, there are words other than look-a-likes, you can ring the changes halfway through by reading out the English meanings instead.
- The checker however still gives the answers in the target language.

To start with, you may be surprised at the number of pupils who have difficulty in locating the correct printed word from a list of six to eight words. You may have to say the words very slowly indeed and repeat them more than once. Even then less able pupils will take an inordinate amount of time spotting the correct word, especially if there are a couple of words with similar spellings, e.g. *chaussettes/chaussures/chemise*. One teacher into whose lesson I introduced this exercise, was shocked to discover the number of pupils who were having difficulty. She commented 'No wonder some of them can't find their way round a page of the textbook. I must sound so fast to them. They can have no idea what words to look for, to match what I'm saying.'

Bright children seem to have little difficulty in doing this exercise, so appoint them as the 'readers aloud'. The middle-of-the-road pupil and the less able pupil should be appointed as 'checkers'.

The next stage is to listen and write. You read out a list of words in the target language and the pupils have to write them down.

And finally they have to be able to produce the correct target language word for either the English or a picture prompt.

Practising look-a-likes has to be continuous throughout the five-year period. In Key Stage 4 I have found brochures and other forms of realia very useful. I have even used a paper placemat from Mc Donald's with a Year 10 SEG group. All the food on offer was pictured on it, each clearly labelled. The task was to practise their French accents by ordering a snack. It took them a good deal of effort and concentration to say 'Chicken McNuggets', 'Milkshake' and 'Cheeseburger' in an acceptable French accent!

##  WHEN AND HOW OFTEN?

Pupils come into our lessons with English ringing in their ears and minds. Professor Eric Hawkins dubbed foreign language teaching '*Gardening in the gale of English*' (Hawkins, 1981).

How do we move our pupils into a non-English thinking environment? If we were to start off every lesson with a number of brief but active listening exercises, their minds and ears would be re-focused on the target language. If we regularly asked them to spend the first five minutes in such activities, we would achieve not only a clear and obvious start to each lesson, but also the habit of moving from one language to the other.

These warm-ups should comprise old as well as new and recently learnt vocabulary and structures. The emphasis of the skills being focused on should move from:

- sound/sight recognition;
- matching meaning;
- accurately writing down (sound prompt);
- accurate recall (picture prompt).

> **!** *T*ake time out and use the first five minutes of a lesson on aural warm-ups!

An excellent activity which combines listening and speaking and makes a good start to a lesson is aural dominoes.

### AURAL DOMINOES

Why these work, I'm not sure. But they do. I have used them for both practising new words and revising old vocabulary from Year 7 to Year 11, using English with the target language or a picture with the target language. I have even used them to practise GCSE oral questions using only target language.

The dominoes can be made on an ordinary word processor or DTP and printed out onto computer labels. The trick is to create a format with known areas, into which the words/sentences can be written, so that when printed they fit neatly onto each label. After printing out, the labels can be peeled off and stuck onto ordinary cardboard. I use off-cuts from either a local printer or the school's own reprographics centre. This way you achieve a durable resource that can be shared between classes.

CILT

If you are into disposable resources — print them out onto paper, cut them up, hand them out but don't expect to get a complete set back in a re-usable condition!

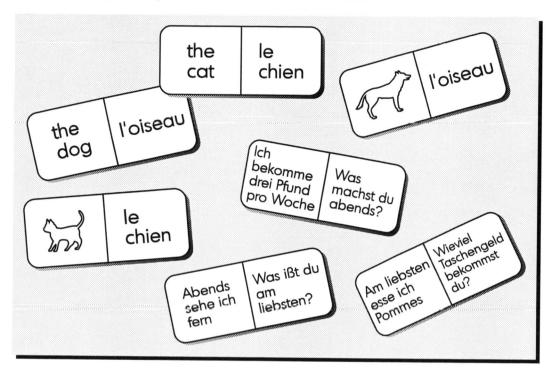

- You will need one domino per pupil in the class. Any absentees' cards have to be either held by the teacher — which can make life quite busy! — or handed as extras to pupils, especially those you want to keep on their toes.
- Hand out the dominoes making sure that they are going out in random order.
- Then point to any pupil and ask them to call out the word/s in the target language e.g. *'Le chien!'*
- The pupil who has the domino with either the English word 'dog' or the picture of the dog, stands up and calls out 'dog!' and then reads out their own TL word *'L'oiseau!'*.
- The pupil with the word or picture of a bird, stands up and calls out 'bird!' and then reads out their own target language word *'Le cheval'*.
- Continue like this round the class until all words have been called.
- Repeat but this time keep a check on the time it takes to complete the round of vocabulary.
- Repeat once more but encourage them to try and beat their own record of X minutes.
- By the third go any pupil daydreaming, not listening, not coming up with their response quickly enough for the likings of their fellow pupils will either be pre-empted and have their answer called out by the others or be nudged into answering by neighbours.
- Have another couple of goes at the end of the lesson, each time trying to lower the time it takes to complete the round.

In the next lesson reverse the process and have the English called out first and see if that speeds up the process.

I believe the benefit of this exercise lies somewhere in the practice it gives both ears and eyes. Having the answer in front of you, allows you to anticipate the question. Even if you don't know how to say the TL word exactly, you stand a good chance at recognising it when someone else says it.

I tried out the GCSE oral question dominoes on a teacher who was herself learning German. She said that it became very easy to hear the word in the question which matched the visual content of her answer.

| | |
|---|---|
| 'Was machst du **abends**?' | '**Abends** sehe ich fern' |
| 'Was ißt du **am liebsten**?' | '**Am liebsten** esse ich Pommes.' |
| 'Was für **Musik hör**st du **am liebsten**?' | '**Am liebsten höre** ich Pop**musik.**' |
| '**Um** wieviel **Uhr steh**st du **auf**?' | 'Ich **steh**e **um** sieben **Uhr auf.**' |

The same cards can be used in extension work by groups. We've found that pupils can have up to six cards each to look at and still be able to respond quickly to questions heard. So a group of five pupils round a table could make use of about 30 dominoes to practise quick-fire questions and answers.

Two side benefits of this exercise are the opportunity it gives teachers to help pupils with pronunciation and the frequency by which all the new words are heard within a short space of time. Fellow pupils are not as tolerant as teachers of poor pronunciation and if there is a break in the chain of rapid fire answers because someone has not said the TL prompt word clearly enough to be understood, then a barrage of correction will be fired by the rest of the class. Far from being discouraging, results would appear to point to the fact that peer judgement is very motivating indeed.

## USING TAPES

No language course would be complete without tapes and the exercises they offer. But bearing in mind all that has already been suggested about the linguistic chaos of the initial learner's mind and the lack of skills in being able to interpret such vital things as word breaks, phrases and the use of intonation, one has to ask how useful disembodied sound is at the beginning of any topic when the new words and structures are still being introduced. At least with video there are all the visual contexts and clues that help in understanding ordinarily what is being said. But a tape is just a stream of sound once again — without the benefit of gesture, facial expression or background.

The recommendation is — and it is one followed by some coursebooks — that pupils look at the tapescript as they listen so that they can follow the sound by reading simultaneously.

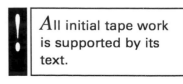

*A*ll initial tape work is supported by its text.

CiLT

And the tape should not just be played through once. Pupils should be given the opportunity to listen and read and re-listen and re-read until they are able to close their eyes, listen and 'see' the words running past in their minds eye; until the tape can be stopped at any point, the text turned to and the place located.

If no text exists in the coursebook, then it is worth every effort it takes to type it up from the teacher's resource book and make copies. If funds are tight and photocopying strictly limited, then a single copy for the OHP could be the answer. Use one pupil at each run through to stand by the OHP and point to the words as they are heard.

How often you will have to play a single tape exercise until your pupils can follow the words, will depend on them. Do not take it for granted that all pupils can do this straight away. You will need to experiment. Some pupils have 'good ears', others do not.

One way of checking how much has been gained is to follow a listening exercise like this with the flash card label exercise mentioned at the beginning of this chapter. For the final play of the tape, hand out labels to the pupils and see whether and how quickly they can identify their word with the sound.

Many tape exercises are not extensive texts; instead they are listening tests. The chunk of language listened to in order to elicit the answer may be no longer than two to three seconds. That does not give the untrained brain much time to disassociate itself from the English sounds rolling around in its thoughts and to refocus on the target language. Nor would you want to have tapescripts if you are looking for answers! The solution here is to warm-up the ear by playing the whole test through at least twice without stopping, before asking pupils to engage in the test.

## MAKING OPPORTUNITIES

Although the emphasis in this book is on the initial learning stages when existing skills are being re-developed and new skills gradually built up, it cannot be repeated often enough that it takes a long time to establish new skills and an even longer time before they become automatic and can be used without conscious effort. To this end exercises and opportunities to practise skills have to continue on a regular basis throughout the learning period.

Regular aural warm-up exercises at the beginning of lessons have been recommended and other suggestions will be made in later chapters. Teachers should be looking to have a battery of prepared exercises that they can turn to — almost at a moment's notice — either to fill in the odd two or three minutes at the end of a lesson or to practise something in particular that has been noticed as a common error. As the pupil becomes more and more adept, so should these exercises expand and develop, until you get to the point where exercises such as the following can be done well by the majority of the pupils at the drop of a hat — unprepared and out of context.

# SOUNDS SIMPLE

On small sheets of paper print out half a dozen rows of words, each horizontal row having similar sounding words.

| bouton | bouteille | au bout | bouche | boue | bouge |
|--------|-----------|---------|--------|------|-------|
| chaise | chère | choix | chef | chaîne | |
| tente | trente | train | tant | tranche | |

| für | fahren | führen | vor | fürchten | | |
|-----|--------|--------|-----|----------|---|---|
| Weise | wieder | weiden | Wiese | weilen | Brüder | |
| Apfel | Brüder | drücken | Äpfel | Druck | | |

- Pupils do **not** have had to have met these words before.
- The aim is to test the pupils' feel for language and knowledge of TL orthography and phonics.
- Starting with the first row, call out a word at a time and pupils have to number the words in the order they hear them.
- Check as you go row by row.

Exercises like this can be pre-prepared as there is no need for the vocabulary to be known. They can of course include some known words. They can be used at any juncture — as fun exercises or as evaluation tests. They can also be extended to the next skill level, whereby you call out a word and the pupils write it down, using their knowledge of orthography to achieve correct or approximate spelling.

When your pupils are able to achieve tests like this with little effort, you know you will have arrived at the point where you can begin to relax. You know that they can now process sound in the target language and 'see' it as a specific word, which they can select from a number given or attempt to spell. They won't be perfect yet — but at least they are on their way.

# 3.    The listening eye

It is as important to train the eye to 'hear' words when read, as it is to 'see' words when heard. Both of these skills stem from activities that are not natural but learnt. A toddler cannot visualise words because it does not know they exist. It cannot make sense of the black 'squiggles' in its favourite bed-time book, because as yet it does not know how to connect the correct sound to each word and so read them.

So, as you re-train the pupils' ears to 'see' words inside their heads, you also need to be re-training the eye to 'hear' them when they are being read. If we don't, we may well be impeding the progress of our pupils.

In class we obviously use those learning techniques that we believe to be effective — otherwise we wouldn't use them. However the most surprising, unforeseen pitfalls can be revealed in discussions with pupils. One Year 8 boy who was causing constant disruption in a class, explained his behaviour in this way.

| | |
|---|---|
| me | Why do you muck around so much in class? |
| him | I don't like French |
| me | Why not? |
| him | Cos it's hard |
| me | Why's it hard? |
| him | Cos you've got to learn lots of words |
| me | What's hard about learning lots of words? |
| him | They don't sound the same when I get them home. |

All I could do was totally agree with him! Why should a pupil who has only a rudimentary feeling for the sound of this new language, be able to carry home with him the correct sound for a dozen or so words?

And yet we hand out lists of words or ask pupils to copy them down into backs of books or vocabulary books in order to 'learn' them at home. I wonder how many pupils in Year 7, when doing this kind of homework, **can** actually hear the correct target language sound of the words they are learning.

It may be that we have hit on yet another possible reason why the sight of the spelling of target language words is thought to have such an effect on children's pronunciation. Could it be because, when they learn them, they are saying the words to themselves using English sounds? Because we have asked them to commit vocabulary to memory before we have satisfactorily fixed target language sound in their minds? They learn badly because we ask them to learn off by heart too soon.

So the first suggestion in this chapter is:

 *D*on't ask for vocabulary to be memorised too soon.

## LEARNING VOCABULARY

If they are made to learn vocabulary off by heart before they have established good aural recall, then it will not come as a surprise to hear the words being spoken in an English accent. We should never give them this homework unless we can ensure that we send both the sound and sight home with them. This was of course the solution to the Year 8 boy's problem given above. The teacher recorded all the vocabulary to be learnt on to a short tape and the boy was put in charge of the departmental dubbing machine. Any pupil could bring in a tape and he would copy the vocabulary on to it. No one in future need go home without the sight and sound of words to be learnt.

If we do ask pupils to read or refer to the printed word before they can hear the words ringing in their ears, then we should expect that they will develop an incompetency rather than a competency. They will read the target language in the same way as they read their own language, translating it into sound using their own established phonics. Or worse. They could do what some of us do when we meet not easily pronouncible foreign words . . . read them silently. That is — we gloss over them.

## JUST A STRING OF LETTERS?

I call it Russian Name syndrome. Unless we have a knowledge of Russian or the name itself is well known or easy to pronounce (Olga, Ivan, Boris), then we will tend to recognise them as a string of letters, a set spelling: Vorotyntsev, Smyslovsky, Nechvobdov. However often we might see them, we may still have difficulty saying them aloud or remembering them well enough to write them down unaided once away from the book. Some of us may try to say the words; most of us will recognise them as a recurring set of letters without sound and pass over quickly.

If you have ever toured in Wales and have not the slightest idea about Welsh pronunciation, you will have almost certainly experienced the same situation there. How would you say the following to yourself if you met them for the first time in a brochure or on a map : Penrhyndeudraeth or Llanfairynghornwy or Machynlleth. And if you were giving directions to these places, what would you say to your driver?

We need to make absolutely sure that our pupils are developing an awareness of target language phonics and that this is encouraged, developed and tested by constant reading aloud. We should continue this as an integral part of learning until they reach the stage where they can read independently and accurately — unaided and unprompted by us.

## TAKING IT STEP BY STEP

If, as suggested in the previous chapter, you are supporting the sound of the new language with the sight of the new words, then it should follow that the next step is to see how much has been taken on board and whether the sight of the words can now recall their sound.

If you have been doing listening exercises with either written labels or a short text and your pupils have been able to locate the words you say with ease, you can be justifiably confident that the sound and sight of those words are successfully fixed in their mind's eye.

But can they now produce the sound of the word from sight? Like many retrieval processes from the brain, it is not an all-or-nothing situation. It is a skill that will develop gradually in most pupils. The NC MFL level descriptions map out clearly the progressive steps anticipated between levels 1–4 in learning to say words.

- Is their 'pronunciation . . . approximate' and do they still need '. . . considerable support from a spoken model' — Attainment Target 2 : Speaking: Level 1
- Or can they manage with less support but still not be entirely confident: 'pronunciation may still be approximate and the delivery hesitant'? — Attainment Target 2 : Speaking: Level 2
- Or are they already at the next step — can they do it without a spoken prompt from you: 'they use mainly memorised language'? — Attainment Target 2 : Speaking: Level 3
- Can they read the labels out loud? — Attainment Target 3: Reading: Level 2
- Are they already showing evidence of Level 4 behaviour as 'their pronunciation is generally accurate'?

If they do need a spoken prompt — Level 1 — then they are still at imitation stage; they have not yet developed the 'internal' sound recall.

If they are hesitant but having a 'go' — Level 2 — then you know they have moved on but are still not yet at that stage where they can confidently reproduce sound on their own, i.e. speak independently — Level 3 — and accurately — Level 4.

What is important for us to remember is that, if they haven't yet developed internal sound recall, then they won't be able to 'hear' the sound of words taken home to learn and so will need other support, such as a tape.

This ability to read words aloud is a vital stage in the initial language learning process. We have to make sure, before we 'push on' with our planned course, that our pupils are capable of this, that they really can produce the correct sounds for words — unaided.

If we don't, if we continue regardless, our pupils will find progress harder and harder to achieve. If they are learning words without the correct sound attached, then either they are learning them silently — as a string of letters — or they are learning them with mother-tongue phonics. Either way, when they are listening to the target language, they will not recognise in the sounds they hear the word they are supposed to have learnt, nor when they are trying to speak will they be able to conjure up the right pronunciation.

## CHECKING PROGRESS

If you adopt the idea of warm-up exercises at the beginnning of the lesson, it gives you an ideal opportunity to keep track of pupils' progress in independent speaking.

Start the lesson by handing out a set of aural dominoes and play a round. Collect in the dominoes, shuffle and re-distribute. Play another round. Repeat for a third time. If no pupil stumbles over or mispronounces any of the words or phrases they have to read, then you have evidence enough that your pupils can match sound to the sight of the written word successfully and have obviously developed a good internal 'ear'.

If they read them *à l'anglaise* or find it impossible without a prompt from you, then it is obvious they still have some way to go. What is more, they are still not at the stage where they can be left to learn words or phrases correctly for themselves.

There is a reason for doing this at the beginning of the lesson. If they are capable of reading aloud unaided at the beginning of a lesson, when they haven't had a chance yet to accustom their ears and eyes to the target language, then they must be really competent.

## STEPS TOWARDS SPEAKING

Of course there will be a grey area as in any process of learning. The sound can be heard in the head, but the confidence to try and reproduce it is lacking. Just a nudge in the right direction is often enough to boost performance. If some pupils' reading is a bit hesitant or not up to their normal standard, then return to the dominoes after doing ten or twenty minutes work. Has the aural input during that time done anything to shake up and re-focus their ability to reproduce sound? The answer will be hopefully: Yes.

When pupils are reading aloud, if they make mistakes, don't give them the correct sound to imitate immediately. Repeat their pronunciation with a querying tone of voice. This may be enough to jog their memory and their second attempt maybe nearer the mark or even spot-on. This is because the right information may be lodged in the brain; it may be just a matter of strengthening the lines of retrieval. To treat all errors as revealing inability does a great disservice to those trying to learn.

## INCORRECT ISN'T NECESSARILY ENTIRELY WRONG

One stage of poor retrieval skills that many pupils go through can be clearly pinpointed by the fact that they retrieve the right letters but they put them in the wrong order.

In one of the English examples given in Chapter 2, a pupil had written down the task instruction as 'Wright a senten to a penfirend'.

- 'Wright' is a unnecessarily complicated grapheme, possibly resulting from a merger between 'write' and 'right'. But at least it successfully reproduces the correct sound.
- 'A senten' is probably misheard. The task was not to write a single sentence. Was it possibly ' Write eight sentences'?
- But 'penfirend' cannot be said to reproduce the intended sound. It is more likely evidence of muddled retrieval.

The word has probably been encountered for the first time in school rather than in life outside. It has been learnt; the letters are there inside the head, but unfortunately, when they are retrieved, they reappear in the wrong order. As no automatic checking of writing appears to be going on, the mind moves onto the next activity and the error goes unnoticed. How many of our pupils are experiencing this when they write '*chein*' or '*souer*' '*zhen*' or '*zwie*'?

We can all recognise this state of not looking at what we are writing; we are often thinking way ahead of the actual words we are writing. Some people become confused and they start to add words or parts of words being thought to words being written. Or they jump from the beginning of one sentence to the end of another and as a result they telescope ideas. They think they have written a complete sentence because the words have gone through their brain. But in fact they have actually missed words out. This can also apply to letters within words; both appear in this example: '*Ma maison est assez grade. Ma chambre. Nous avons une cuisine . . .*' (Year 8 pupil)

This extract from what was otherwise an extended piece of writing with remarkably few errors, reveals an interruption to the line of thought. Perhaps he was distracted by something, perhaps he daydreamed for a few minutes; whatever the cause the result is clear. That the misspelling 'grade' is not through lack of knowledge but through a momentary lapse in attention becomes clear later on when he is capable of writing: '*Nous avons deux assez grands jardins*'.

The '*grade*' is well thought through enough to have the correct feminine agreement. The loss of the '*n*' and then subsequently the entire meaning of the next sentence beginning '*Ma chambre*' can be put down to a severe lapse in concentration and, what is more important, is evidence that **the pupil did not re-read what he had written.** Had he done so, the omissions would surely have been picked up.

## THE BENEFITS OF BEING ABLE TO READ ALOUD

It sounds such an obvious statement: He should have re-read what he had written, then the omissions, i.e. errors, would have been picked up. Children are probably encouraged to do this from their earliest schooldays. But why? Why is the re-reading of writing an effective means of spotting errors?

> **!** *D*evelop the habit of checking what they write with what they can hear inside their heads.

I believe that reading aloud, whether externally or internally, works as a means of checking for mistakes and omissions because the brain's ability to store is better than our conscious ability to retrieve. By matching the one against the other we can immediately spot errors, whether misspellings or omissions or words in the wrong order — all those kind of mistakes that low levels of concentration when writing might cause.

Apochryphal stories abound in staff rooms of whole classes copying down complete nonsense from the board and only realising their mistake when one of them is asked to read the text aloud. The mind is not necessarily engaged when one is copying writing. The mind, as we have seen above, can be easily distracted when writing. But in order to re-read aloud what has been written, one's eyes need to follow the words as they appear. If these are sounded out, either aloud or internally, then misspellings, poor structuring and omissions seem to leap from the page. Time and time again I have seen pupils correct their own work, just because they have been encouraged to re-read it aloud. This must indicate that the brain has stored somewhere the correct pattern of sound or cadence of the sentence structure and the correct 'look' of the word and the act of reading aloud gives the brain the chance to match the two.

Perhaps this ability or skill is linked to one of those miraculous skills of the brain that cannot as yet be fully explained, namely the ability to immediately spot when a note is played off-key during an unknown piece of music. Apparently one does not even have to be musical to be able to do this. It cannot be that our brains are programmed to understand all music before it is heard, just that we are acutely aware aurally of what is possible or probable as a following sound.

I should imagine in our early years of listening we develop quite a sound basis for something similar in our own language, so that we know, seemingly instinctively by the time we begin to talk, that 'the big' cannot be followed by 'ate' and that 'the boys are . . .' cannot be followed by 'ran' but 'running'.

In those vital initial stages of foreign language learning, by listening to, and therefore inputting into our brains, the sound of target language words, phrases and sentences, we are building up an aural store of pattern and intonation and cadence and a visual store of spellings on which we can later rely.

So we should be giving pupils plenty of opportunity to listen to the sound of the language and to repeat sounds and structures aloud — either internally or externally. What is more, we should be encouraging them to use this store of sound as their first port of call when checking their own work.

## BUILDING THE INNER EAR

Pupils should be encouraged to recall and practise sound in their head before they say a word or phrase or a sentence aloud. This can be easily achieved in class and should become a regular instruction.

*Répète le mot à voix basse/ à toi*          *Sag das Wort innerlich*

*Tu peux entendre le mot dans ta tête?*     *Kannst du das Wort innerlich hören?*

## DISCRIMINATING SOUNDS

Pupils need to practise seeing a word or phrase and selecting the right sound for it. This exercise makes excellent use of a machine like the Language Master, where blank cards, i.e. with no visual prompt at all, can be recorded with single words or phrases. The pupils are given a list of words or phrases to find and have to play the

*Picture of LM with cards clearly showing magnetic strips*

CiLT

various blank cards through the machine. They set aside those with the sounds that match the words on the list. As pupils become better at 'hearing' words, 'red herrings' should be recorded to distract them. Some of these can be the same as written versions being used to distract in the listening exercises illustrated in the previous chapter, i.e. *Il m'appelle   Je l'appelle.*

If only tape recorders are available to you, a similar exercise can be created on tape. Pupils have a numbered list of words or phrases. On the tape are some of the words only. Pupils have to listen and tick whether they are hearing the right sound for that number.

## POINTING OUT MISTAKES

There is nothing pupils like better than correcting a teacher. So encourage the following:

- using a well rehearsed list of vocabulary or a text from a coursebook, begin reading aloud, deliberately mispronouncing some of the words;
- pupils have to shout out '*Erreur!*' or '*Falsch!*' whenever they hear a word mis-pronounced.

This is an especially useful exercise if you make use of mispronunciations that you have heard pupils use or you exaggerate any prevailing English accents.

The next best thing to correcting a teacher is correcting a friend. So once they have corrected you, ask one of them to do the reading aloud. If you don't like the idea of encouraging pupils to make deliberate errors, remember — to intentionally make a mistake, you have to be very aware of **what is right.** Try it out with older pupils first. They won't find it easy.

## THE 'BLACKBOARD OF THE BRAIN'

The importance of developing internal sound and vision during the early stages of language learning cannot be underestimated A research programme that was included in the Channel 4 *Mystery of the senses* programme revealed the following.

A woman was placed in a scanner, so that the activity of her brain could be monitored and recorded. She was then read a list of simple items such as 'Apple. Bird. Ball. Dog . . . ', etc; she had to imagine the object, i.e. 'see' it in her imagination and say 'yes' as soon as the image was clear in her mind. Then the same list was re-read, but this time she was shown a picture of each item as the name was read out. So now her brain was having to match the sight of an object with the sound of its name, rather than just locate the meaning and the image of a sound within her brain.

What was remarkable was that the activity pattern of the brain hardly differed during the two exercises. When conjuring up the image of each word into her imagination, that part of the brain that controls sight was as fully active as when it was consciously matching an externally seen object with the sound of the word. The conclusion drawn was that internal sight is as much 'seeing' as external sight.

This is important for us, because as language teachers we have to build up a new system of word recognition in the target language so that:

- pupils can recognise words externally, i.e. when reading; and
- so they can recall words accurately, when they want to say or write them.

If the same part of the brain is responsible for both, then by developing the one, we may well be simultaneously developing the other. If we can recall accurately a word to our mind's eye, then we will have no difficulty in recognising that same word when we see it externally. When we see it externally, we should be able to recognise whether or not it is spelt correctly by checking it against the internal version.

I have always referred to this ability to 'see' in the mind's eye as 'the blackboard of the brain'. I used to ask my pupils to very deliberately write words and phrases to be learnt on this 'blackboard'. When recalling words or meanings, I would ask them to shut their eyes and write the word letter by letter or draw the picture on this inner space as a deliberate step in the retrieval process. This can be a useful ploy to pass on to pupils who are having difficulty learning new words. It can also be very revealing.

I once worked with a class where a boy always put his hand up in immediate response to any question put by the teacher. However, if he was asked to answer, he would mumble and look embarrassed and say he'd forgotten what he was going to say. After observing this several times, I decided to investigate. It turned out that he had severe learning problems. He could not recall any word of more than three letters. He was in fact learning very little indeed and, to mask this, he pretended to be paying attention and offering to answer. Apparently his excuses for non-appearance of homework were as convincing as the performance he had been putting on in class. Within half a term he had improved to the point where he could recall and spell words of up to six letters — which extended his vocabulary somewhat!

## REVERSING THE PROCESS

Many of the exercises suggested in Chapter 2 can be extended so that the listening and matching exercises are immediately followed by reading aloud exercises

**The list game:** as already suggested, as soon as pupils show themselves adept at picking out words as you sound them, hand over the selection to them and get them to call out the words.

**Look-a-likes:** This needs years of practice. Hand out a list of new look-a-like vocabulary; ask the pupil/s to practise by themselves silently; then, ask for volunteers to read the words aloud as they think they should be pronounced. As the correct sound has not yet been heard, they have to dig deep into their experience and the sounds stored in their brains to do this activity.

This same principle can also work as a group or pair activity. The pupils individually record themselves saying the new words as best they can; then, as a group or as a pair, they listen to a master tape with the correct pronunciations. They then replay their own recordings and have to judge who in their opinion came closest to the correct sound.

**The stand-up sit-down game:** instead of standing up and sitting down as you hear a single word, you have more than one word or phrase on cards. These are turned over as they are heard. This exercise can then be followed by a gapfill exercise in which the teacher pauses in the story and the pupil who holds that card, fills in the gap orally.

The same can be achieved using **tapescripts:** when replaying a tape for the third or fourth time, turn the volume down from time to time and ask the class or individuals to continue reading aloud.

**Practising phonics:** using material similar to the *Bouche/bouge/bougie/bout/bouteille* exercise, pupils have to select the correct written words from a selection while listening to a tape of the words or phrases. This could be just isolated words or phrases or you could create a complete but brief text which they have to recreate with the word cards. They then reverse the process and re-read aloud the words, phrases or text they have assembled. If another pupil is following the original tape with the headphones half on half off, then any words a pupil stumbles over can be quickly supplied by the other.

Throughout the early stages of learning, it should be made clear to the pupils that you are not expecting them to achieve perfection immediately, that developing an ear and eye for a new language is not something that will be theirs overnight. Only through dint of practice and more practice will their brains be able to sort out what they need to know . You may like to reassure them that once the skills have been developed, then learning will speed up, become easier and more accurate. The benefits may take some time coming, but in the end they will be worth it.

# 4.    Storage and recall

It is only when pupils can recognise the sound of new vocabulary, attach the correct meaning to it, locate it within text and then read the written version aloud, that they should be entrusted with the learning of it off by heart. Otherwise too many existing automatic procedures of thought may interfere with their learning.

This means that in the initial stages we ought to be spending much longer than we usually do developing and practising the receptive skills of listening and reading before moving on to the productive skills of speaking and writing . One of the constant cries of all teachers in the classroom to any new methodology is 'But there isn't time!'. What is being suggested here really is a case of '*Il faut reculer pour mieux sauter*'. If we take time in the early stages to develop the necessary skills, if we can train our pupils in good learning techniques early on, then as their skills develop and become more practised, we can reduce the amount of time spent on such things without sacrificing the quantity and quality of learning.

In the Programme of Study Part 1, 3a and 3b state that pupils should be taught to:

**a**   Learn by heart phrases and short extracts,
e.g. rhymes, poems, songs, jokes, tongue twisters;

**b**   acquire strategies for committing familiar language to memory.

Note that they say commit 'familiar language to memory'; obviously they are not expecting pupils to be asked to learn off by heart vocabulary that they have only just be introduced to.

 ## HOW DO PUPILS LEARN?

I wonder if you have ever asked your pupils how they learn their vocabulary. I began to do this on a regular basis with pupils in both Key Stages, after I had listened to pupils in Key Stage 4 who were utterly disenchanted with foreign language learning, who were making very little effort and who were threatening to give up on the subject altogether. I asked one of them what the problem was:

| | |
|---|---|
| pupil | There are so many words I don't understand |
| me | How many new words do you teach yourself every week? |
| pupil | (in amazement) What? What do you mean? |
| me | How many words do you learn a week? |
| pupil | Depends on what we're doing in class — I suppose. |
| me | What do you mean? When do you learn new words? |
| pupil | I just pick them up in class. |
| me | And is that enough? Can you expect to understand just by picking words up in class? How many new words or phrases do you think you should be learning every week? |

CiLT

There then followed a general class discussion about how large a vocabulary would be needed to get through GCSE and how many words would you have to learn per week over the five years to have a good enough vocabulary (the answer is ten to fifteen!). But the pupil was still complaining:

| pupil | But they're hard to learn! |
| me | Why? How do you learn them? |
| pupil | I look at the paper they're written on. |
| me | And . . ? |
| pupil | Well . . . I look at them . . . I take the paper out . . . maybe two . . . three times in an evening and look at them. |
| me | And that's enough? You can learn them like that? |
| pupil | Oh no! I don't learn them like that. That's why it's hard. |
| me | Then why do you go on doing it like that? Why don't you do something else? |
| pupil | (surprised) How else can you learn them? |

Her friends immediately started telling her how they learnt their vocabulary. Their methods ranged from writing them out over and over again to getting a friend or family to test them. The pupil complaining was quite surprised. It apparently had not dawned on her in four years of language learning that to continue with a method of learning that wasn't working, was pointless. The idea of changing her method had never crossed her mind. Perhaps she had never had her attention drawn to various other possible ways of learning. Perhaps it had never been discussed before; it had just been taken for granted that from the age of eleven onwards she would know how to learn off by heart. What was more saddening was the fact that her poor methods of learning had resulted in her being judged as a natural and 'for ever' poor learner and no extra effort appeared to have been made to make her a better one.

## ARE YOU AN EARS OR AN EYES PERSON?

The means and methods people use to install information in their brains are about as varied as people themselves. Some people — very few — appear to take on board effortlessly all they can see and hear. They can reproduce it faultlessly from the word Go and make use of it immediately. Some put this down to having a photographic memory; others show almost total aural recall. But they are few and far between. Most of us need to make an effort.

There are broadly two different schools of methodology — those that like to listen to words and recall aurally and those that like to see or write the word and recall visually. And there is a large percentage in the middle who use a bit of both. So any common learning method applied in class should encompass both these opportunities. Either the written work should be well supported by sound or the aural work well supported by text. At times, though, individual exercises may tend more to one than the other, as in the fan-fold method mentioned below. But if the learning off by heart is delayed until such times as the sight and sound have been welded together by constant practice and reinforcement, then, whatever the pupil does in order to impress vocabulary into its memory, we will have minimised the threat of the written word not being attached to sound or the heard word not being attached to the correct written word.

What follows presumes that vocabulary has been introduced to the class, has been practised, played around with, reinforced and that the skills discussed in the two previous chapters are now in place. Depending on the class ability and the favoured methodology of the teacher, more or less time may have been spent getting pupils to a point where you feel that the learning by heart can now take place.

###  ON THE LOOK-OUT FOR ERROR

> **!** *D*o not trust the copying skills of your pupils.

The first suggestion is, when the class is writing new words down for learning off by heart, walk around the classroom and check, check, check! However often you may have said the words, however often they might have seen the words, when they come to copy them down, whether into an exercise book or a vocabulary book or whatever, you still have to check — as they are writing — what they are writing.

I have watched a Year 8 pupil dispense with common sense and believe that his eyes were reading '*géagraphie*' from an OHT, rather than suppose that the teacher had made a mistake — actually the writing was small and the OHP pen rather too blobby. When I asked him to check what he had written, he still read the OHT as saying '*géagraphie*'. When I asked him if it was likely that the word 'geography' would suddenly change its spelling like that, he replied: 'It's French, so it might.' A perfectly reasonable answer for someone who has never been introduced to the influence of Greek roots on European vocabulary or who has not had the similarities/differences between French and English vocabulary highlighted. When I asked him how it was pronounced, he was able to say the word correctly and yet he still maintained that it could be spelt '*géa . . .*' even when sounding like '*géo . . .*'

Constantly monitoring pupils' work as they produce it and querying errors as they occur, has often provided me with pupils' most revealing misconceptions — ideas that would never have dawned on a teacher and the written evidence of which would normally be put down to poor learning, rather than a misunderstanding.

It is a fact that in the early stages of second and foreign language learning pupils can be creating the weirdest and wildest theories and hypotheses about the new language they are tackling. Many of these are caused by a single concept, one shared by many, if not most, learners of foreign languages.

> *The naive learner beginning his first foreign language lesson starts from the hypothesis that the foreign language basically functions in the same way as his own language with only the lexical items being different.*
>
> (Ringbom, 1987)

We have all seen the results of this belief — transliteration. It is especially common during pupils' first efforts at free writing.

'*Ich bin gehen*' for 'I am going'        '*je suis onze ans*' for 'I am 11'
'*Ich bin heisse*' for ' I am called'     '*mein Bruder's Zimmer*' for 'my brother's room'

In extreme cases it can override the evidence of their own eyes and make them read what they think they are seeing, rather than what is actually there.

During the summer term, i.e. after two terms of learning, during which time the following phrases must have been seen, copied, said and written umpteen times, I watched a very bright Year 7 pupil copy down a dialogue from the board like this:

> *Bonjour! Je'm appelle Marie. Et toi?*
> *Bonjour. Je'm appelle Luc. Tu as des frères ou des soeurs?*
> *Oui. J'ai un frère. Il's appelle Jean. J'ai une soeur. Elle's appelle Anne.*

At this point I asked the pupil to check what he had written with what was on the board. He did so and couldn't see anything wrong. As I knew he knew about apostrophes and their uses, I asked him to check these in particular. He did so and still couldn't see anything wrong. I then pointed out the misplaced apostrophes and explained why they were needed where they should be. He replied:

> 'Oh. I thought it was like the English. 'I'm called' so '*Je'm appelle*'. I'm = *Je'm*
> And the same here . . . '*Il's appelle*' is 'He's called'. He's = *Il's* . . .'

I wonder how many mistakes made by our pupils have as conscious a reason behind them as that. Uncorrected, he would soon have been retrieving from his memory '*Je'm grand*' in the same way the pupil mentioned in Chapter 1 retrieved '*je m'appelle grand*'.

Small wonder then that those pupils who don't even understand what use an apostrophe serves in English can be seen to copy them down at random or even, which I have very commonly observed, mistake them for commas or accents and vice versa.

> *Il,'sappelle*     *J'mapple*     *Je'mappelle*     *J' mappelle*     *Je ' m appelle*
> *fre're*          *pe're*         *pre's*          'a or a' ( *for à*)

## CONTROLLING INPUT

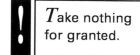

In order to avoid elementary copying errors, I recommend handing out printed lists of words/phrases to be learnt. I print one landscape A4 sheet per pupil with the vocabulary on the left hand side in a neat column. Other lines are printed across the page to create c 8 column spaces.

| | | | | | | | |
|---|---|---|---|---|---|---|---|
| die Maus<br>die Katze<br>der Hund<br>der Vogel<br>das Kaninchen<br>das Pferd | | | | | | | |

Before the sheet goes home, the English meanings are entered into the second column and these are then checked by the whole class to make sure everyone has them down right. In the less able classes I check that the English spellings are correct.

Now the sheet goes home for homework. The technique is known as fan-fold. First column no. 1 is folded over so that only the English meanings in column no. 2 are visible. The pupil writes down as best they can from memory the TL words.

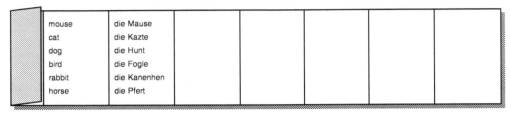

| mouse | die Mause | | | | | | |
|-------|-----------|--|--|--|--|--|--|
| cat | die Kazte | | | | | | |
| dog | die Hunt | | | | | | |
| bird | die Fogle | | | | | | |
| rabbit | die Kanenhen | | | | | | |
| horse | die Pfert | | | | | | |

Having finished, they open up the hidden column, check and correct their answers as necessary. Then columns 1 and 2 are folded over leaving the TL words in column 3 visible. Now the English meanings are written down in column 4. When finished, these are checked and corrected against the information in column 2. And so on across the sheet, folding over one more column each time and entering in alternately TL words and their English meanings.

| die Maus | mouse | die Mause | mouse | die Mause | mouse | die Maus | |
|----------|-------|-----------|-------|-----------|-------|----------|--|
| die Katze | cat | die Kazte | cat | die Katze | cat | die Katze | |
| der Hund | dog | die Hunt | dog | der Hund | dog | der Hund | |
| der Vogel | bird | die Fogle | bird | die Vogel | bird | der Vogel | |
| das Kaninchen | rabbit | die Kanenhen | | die Kaninhen | rabbit | die Kaninchen | |
| das Pferd | horse | die Pfert | horse | das Pferd | horse | das Pferd | |

The sheet is then stuck into the exercise or vocabulary book as a record of learning. The immediate benefit is that a teacher can assure themselves that the learning homework has been done. And the pupils can 'show off' that they have indeed done their homework! This was the surprise result when a set of bottom ability Year 10s were given their first fan-fold homework, in an attempt to remediate their learning skills. They came into the next lesson brandishing their homework, eager to show the teacher that they had 'learnt' their words.

Secondly, pupils with poor copying and checking techniques can be easily spotted when the teacher checks these learning sheets. These pupils will need extra help and guidance before they can be left to do such work alone successfully.

And thirdly, the greater percentage of pupils will have the meanings and the better part of the correct spellings firmly lodged in their heads after this exercise.

cilt

# CALL

> **!** *M*ake use of the unique contribution that the computer can make to learning.

But if given the chance, there is one other activity that I would use before I sent any work home to be learnt — I would try to integrate Computer Assisted Language Learning (CALL) into all Key Stage 3 lessons. For each class I would book approximately 30 minutes in the computer room on a regular basis once a week or once a fortnight — especially during those vital first few terms of language learning.

Since 1983 I have been using a suite of programs with pupils to support and enhance the three steps taken in every topic studied:

**1** Vocabulary learning     **2** Practising structures     **3** Putting both into context.

I will deal with the last two in the following chapters. Here I would just like to look at vocabulary learning and the question of how children learn.

During the first experimental years in the early 80s I tried out any number of computer programs on the market, even adapting some for modern languages that weren't intended as such. I very quickly noticed that a certain vocabulary learning program seemed to be benefitting the pupils — Kosmos' *French Mistress* and *German Master*. My initial observations and conclusions were borne out by subsequent practice. Pupils' behaviour became so predictable that when I became an advisory teacher I knew I could introduce this program to unknown pupils, whose teaching I had not in any way as yet influenced, and yet I could still anticipate their actions and reactions on this program (and some others). Why? It has taken me many more years to unpeel the possible reasons that underpin the important and, I believe, unique contribution the computer can make.

This particular program is pupil friendly — pupils don't appear to mind making mistakes on it — because, as they tell me, 'You can always have another go and get better at it.' This is encouraging and motivating. Instead of setting pupils to compete against each other, the computer encourages them to compete against themselves. Instead of testing them once only and judging their ability on that test, it allows them to go over and over the same test, removing errors until perfection or near perfection is attained.

Pupils can do three things during this program in order to spell the word or phrase required:

- they can enter the letters confidently because they know them and are right;
- they can enter them confidently or less so because they think they know them and are wrong;
- they can decide that they don't know how to start or how to continue to spell a word and ask for a hint by pressing the TAB or COPY key which will fill in the next letter.

Each time they try the exercise, their aim is to decrease the numbers of errors or hints given. I have never met a pupil yet who did not improve in this manner over a 30-minute lesson. They may have made 25 errors and needed 25 hints on their first go, but by the end of the lesson, three or four or more goes later, they are happily recording only four errors and two hints, maybe even a clear round.

No conventional vocabulary test I know of is willingly undertaken by pupils so many times in quick succession, with the express intention of getting fewer errors. But then no conventional vocabulary test informs the pupil immediately that the last letter entered is wrong. No conventional test allows a pupil to be given a word letter by letter until whatever process is occurring in the brain suddenly recalls the rest and the pupil is able to fill in confidently what it can — what it does know.

This program's unique feature is that it gives instantaneous correction. This is one of the two important factors that has made me remain with this program for over fourteen years. Time and time again I have stood behind a group of pupils and listened to them as they try the exercise for a second or third time and heard them say:

'No! Not that! It's an 'e'. Remember you put 'a' last time and we were wrong. It's an 'e'.
or
Don't you remember — we did that last time and nothing happened. It's not right . . . What is then?
I don't know. I'm not sure. But I know it's not that . . .
Try TAB again, 'cos I don't know either.'

I call this the power of negative learning. By allowing pupils to put down what they believe to be right, by telling them at each step of the way whether they are right or not and then letting them repeat the test over and over again so as to eliminate their errors, it becomes clear that the force of immediate correction is a powerful mind-check in all subsequent goes.

It is as if the memory had tagged a certain action or spelling with a large reminder 'Don't do this again!'. Because the correction and the next attempt follow in such close succession, this tag is clearly recalled and the warning noted. As the pupil repeats the exercise a few more times, the warning to avoid a wrong answer appears to become superfluous as the pattern of the correct reply becomes more immediate and then automatic.

It is not surprising then that frequent use of this program sharpens pupils' awareness of accuracy, prevents continuing use of wrong retrieval processes and replaces them with correct procedures which can be developed to such a pitch that they become automatic responses.

When conducting an ordinary, traditional vocabulary test in the class, our corrections may well be made at home that evening and it may be two days before we hand back the work. The mistakes are obvious; they are marked in red or whatever. The corrections are not necessarily so obvious . I have yet to see pupils intently looking at the mistakes and then making a mental note of their errors. Because there is no immediate repeat of the test, no mental 'warning tag' is put against any of the mistakes.

The traditional vocabulary test is by all accounts a very unsatisfactory method of learning — all the more so because to the pupils only 10/10 is a satisfactory result. Even 9/10 or 8/10 is not good enough for them. As for 4/10 or less — well it just goes to show that you're pretty hopeless at this subject, doesn't it?

[When the acknowledging of results is inevitable, I always start from 1 and work upwards. 'Who got one or more right?' 'Two?' 'Three?', etc. And I encourage those who constantly get low marks by saying that 0/10 is what they should get if they hadn't learnt anything. And then I suggest other ways that might make learning more fruitful.]

By using this computer program, I have children crowing with delight because they have reduced the number of errors from 25 to 12. 'I'm going to have another go and get it down to below ten, Miss!' I have watched the change in children who have sat at the back of the class since primary school, quite happily accepting the judgement of their teachers that they are poor learners but who, when put on a computer, have to work, have to actually do something and, in the end, have to think for themselves. They have turned round beaming to report 'Miss, I've only made 30 errors this time . . . down from 65.' Just imagine that pupil's result on a conventional test. It would have confirmed her worst doubts — that she was no good at this subject. Here on the computer 30 errors out of a possible 175 letters instead of 65/175 looks exactly what it is — progress!

The other important factor is the use of the TAB key — the hint. Once again I have frequently witnessed children searching their brains for the spelling of a word which they can say quite happily: they can remember some of it but not all of it.

 ### INCOMPLETE RETRIEVAL

The screen is showing:

The group confidently enter 'm'.
One of them is about to enter 'o' when stopped by another.
'No! Not 'mon'! It's an 'a' — 'ma' 'ma soeur' .
No. 3 agrees and the 'a' is dutifully and correctly entered; as is the 's' of *soeur* and now the fun begins:
'It's 'o' 'u' 'e' 'r', isn't it ' suggests No. 1.
'No, it's 'u''o' 'e' 'r'.' contradicts No. 2.
And No. 3 chips in with ' I'm not sure. Let's TAB it.'

They press the TAB key and the 'o' appears.
'See', says No. 1 triumphantly, 'I was right. Now it's 'u'' and the key is pressed and nothing happens — of course.
'No, it's not. See that's a mistake. Don't do it again. It's wrong!
'What is it then? 's' 'o' . . ?'
'Shall we TAB?' says No. 3, who is obviously very unsure.
'Give me a pencil! Let me write it down.' says No. 1 who still can't quite believe he's wrong.
'I think it's that funny 'e' which we can't do on this computer. Do you remember? . . . but we can write it in our books. It's part of the 'o'. She told us about in class. Try 'e''
No. 1 is not convinced 'Nah! It's not 'e'! Look 's' 'o' 'e' . . . looks dead silly. Try TAB!'

With two out of three now in agreement, TAB is pressed and produces the disputed 'e'.

They have to TAB to get the 'u' as well but are able to finish off with the 'r'.

So their first effort has result in three TAB keys out of five letters. Or to put it more positively 2/5 letters right! They may not be able to spell the word correctly, but they do know all the letters; it's just they can't quite recall the order of them yet.

I have seen children being able to finish off ' frè . . .' having TABbed the 'f', added the 'r', TABbed the 'è' and happily and confidently added 're'.

I have seen children having to TAB 'c' 'o' 'c' 'h' before the brain supplies '-on'.

I have seen them enter 'Il', add an 's' and make, to their suprise, 'Ils'; they then enter *s'appelle* after some deliberation among themselves, but have to TAB in the 'nt'.

This has to be a midpoint in retrieval tactics of the brain. We can 'see' the whole word well enough to get an idea of it and even to say it, but the actual letter by letter recall is less secure — just as in the 'penfirend' example given earlier. However, if pupils can be given what they're not sure of or what they know they don't know, then the filling in of what they do know or think they know becomes an encouraging and positive feature.

In a French children's Playbook bought this summer, I found the following exercise:

```
  p*pe       *renouille      *oleil      lun*        â*e
```

(from *Initiation aux Mots; Gommettes et Jeux:* 5 (éditions fleuris)

Wouldn't this be a comforting first-step exercise for those who are having to develop memorising tactics? For those who, in my experience, need the use of some kind of external 'TAB key' or prompt for some considerable time because either they lack the confidence needed to risk making a mistake, or because they really have had poor learning experiences up till now. Never having been asked to do it before, they find it difficult to suddenly be asked to store and retrieve accurately.

Having practised adding one letter to complete the word, the French activity book then progressed on to adding in syllables.

(from *Initiation aux Mots; Gommettes et Jeux:* 5 (éditions fleuris)

CiLT

Not only does an activity like this reinforce in a pupil's mind where the syllable breaks are in a word, but it may also play a part in the development of recall. Just at that stage where the whole word is stored but the retrieval lines are shaky, not yet well established, we can use exercises like this to jog the recall system into retrieving part of the word.

If pupils can do such exercises, then you can be assured that the storage at least is complete. They have to be retrieving the letter or syllable from somewhere! If they can fill in a letter, good. If they can fill in a whole syllable, better. And if they can give the whole word, great!

The computer program I use allows just this: pupils can fill in the whole word or phrase letter by letter correctly, monitoring each entry as it is made, but they can also TAB in any letter they don't know or are unsure of. Surely it is better to practise in stages rather than expecting accurate off-by-heart recall from everyone after a learning homework, over which we have no control.

## AT ONE'S OWN PACE

And what of the more able child? The child who **does** make the effort to learn accurately or who learns vocabulary **easily**? What happens to her or him on the computer, if after the first go, they achieve no errors and no TABs?

Speed takes over. Once accuracy is achieved, repeating the same exercise over and over again to meet some mythical lowest record time or to keep chipping away at one's own previous time can absorb a pupil to such a degree that when the bell rings for the end of lesson, it is greeted with groans of dismay and cries of ' Can't I just finish this one?' I am content because I know the end result will be of more use to them than any feeling they might have had gaining 10/10 once on a conventional test. I know that when that word or phrase is needed, whether in oral or written work, the recall procedures in the brain, so well honed by constant fast practice, will instantly and accurately spring the correct target language word or phrase to mind.

Having watched children over the last fourteen years being able to retrieve single letters of words, more than one letter, beginning bits or end bits of words before finally the whole word, I am convinced that storage in and retrieval from the brain are two separate things, each of which has to be considered separately.

If the storage or input is accurate, then there is a possibility that eventually recall or output will be accurate. But if the storage or input is incorrect or vague or misunderstood or based on a misconception, then there is no possibilty at all of the recall ever being accurate.

Once we get the activities that correctly store vocabulary right, then the next step is not necessarily immediate total recall. Instead, we should be anticipating that for many of our pupils accurate recall may be an activity that has to be developed. We have to believe that it can be coaxed from even the most reluctant learner by asking for single letter in-fill, multi-letter in-fill, syllable in-fill and finally whole word recall. We can do this with exercises made for use in the classroom or by certain computer programs.

### CHECKING FOR ACCURATE STORAGE

Can we tell when pupils have a word or phrase stored in their heads?

Can they recognise the word when they see it? Can they pick it out from a jumble of others? If they can, then — YES — it must be stored in their heads. Use linear word searches or spelling tables.

### Linear word search 1

> piedtrottinetteavionvoiturechevalautobusbateaucartrainfuséevélohélicoptère

If pupils can see the ends and beginnings of words and can separate them successfully, then they are recognising the whole against some internal mental image of the word. If you don't believe this, try the exercise above on someone who knows no French at all and see where and why they come unstuck!

## Linear word search 2

> trotinetchepiedvioturetrottinetteavionfuseévoiturevelochevaldeautobusabta
> chevabateausecartthélicoptèrehraretrainvèlopeidfuséevoitvéloavointraimer

Move on to linear word search 2 where pupils are deliberately misled by 'almost words' and misspellings.

Exercises like these are much more difficult than those more usual block or square wordsearches. They also have the added advantage of mimicking the lineality of reading, whereas conventional wordsearch squares sometimes hide words diagonally or even backwards!

A third exercise could actual give breaks between supposed words and pupils have to underline those they now recognise.

> trotinet che pied à vioture trottinette est avion fuseé la voiture velo cheval
> de autobus abta les va bateau se cart hélicoptère le hrare train vèlo peid
> fusée voici vélo mon avoin traimer a

Don't be suprised if, for instance, '*a*' '*à*' and '*des*' are ignored. It takes some time before beginners give reading value to anything other than 'information words' as opposed to 'function words'.

Encouraging pupils to look for what they **can** recognise and understand in among a welter of unknown words is a major first step on the way to reading.

CILT

## SPELLING TABLES

I first made these up for the class where the boy was sure that the word was 'geagraphie' and where his friends were copying down words to learn with just as many errors. I noted some of their errors down and next day threw them back at the class as a table of possible spellings. All they had to do was underline the correct spelling.

The results were interesting: a small number each time selected the clearly 'aurally' stored 'listoire' 'onglay' 'fissique'. There was even a small but intensely felt discussion about whether spelling even mattered so long as a word was understood. I asked them to carry that discussion over into their English lesson!

| anglias | desin | listoire | allamend | phsysique |
|---------|-------|----------|----------|-----------|
| anglais | dessign | historie | allemand | physices |
| englais | dissign | histoire | allemend | physique |
| onglay | dessin | histiore | allimand | fissique |

I have since found this a very useful exercise. I take errors made by the pupils themselves in a homework, draw up a table, and hand it out before the books are returned. Pupils then complete the exercise, have their books returned and then check what they actually wrote in their homework.

Sometimes they are horrified at the silly slips that they have made. The spelling table exercise has clearly shown that they are capable of recognising that 'cheveux' is the correct spelling. Why oh why then did they write 'chevuex' last night?

A doubly useful exercise because it makes pupils look at the corrections to work done in a very focused fashion!

It is just as useful with phrases as with words

| | | |
|---|---|---|
| je m'apple | jay abite | j'ai onze ans |
| je' m' appelle | j'ai habit | jay onse an |
| je m'appelle | shabeat | je onze an |
| j' m' appelle | j'habite | jay onze ans |

All these are genuine examples of pupil production at the end of Year 7!

There has been a school of thought for many years that prides itself in never showing mistakes to pupils. Such an exercise would be an anathema to them. I actually think it's very useful. I believe from my experience and observations when watching pupils doing such exercises that the talk generated about accuracy and error is very healthy indeed. And cognitively speaking, the ability to spot a correct spelling from a host of wrong ones can only mean that somewhere inside the brain what is being read outside is being checked inside and matched and found to be OK.

And as the spellings are all theirs anyway, there is a great deal of 'mind jogging' going on. If you hear a fellow pupil scoffing at the mistake you made, the drive to make sure you don't do it again is greater than any red mark made by a teacher.

## CHECKING FOR ACCURACY

Can we check accurate input and recall other than by conventional methods?

Yes. I would always place the emphasis first of all on whole class recall, then team recall, then group and finally individual. I do this by having alphabet cards plus accent cards. A number of pupils volunteer or are selected to come to the front of the class where the ABC cards are. I call out in the target language a word we have been learning and they have to pick out the cards to spell it. The class acts as the checker and points out any mistake by calling 'erreur' or 'falsch'. After a few words I hand over to the pupils and let them call out words. Then a new set of pupils goes up to the front and so on.

The next lesson I will divide the class into two to four teams depending on the size of class; each team will have a set of ABC cards and they now compete against each other to see who can arrange the words correctly fastest.

The same 'game' is then played in subsequent lessons in the usual working groups of four to six pupils, until the point is reached at which the exercise can be done without the ABC cards, i.e. they have to write the word down. They are still at this stage working as a group because this may well still be a stage of partial recall. John can give the beginning bit, Mary chips in with the next letter, Matthew remembers the accent and Simon recalls the end.

It is only after much practice that the 'game' develops into individual response. Previously known as a vocabulary test, it will now appear instead as a game. Its gradual build-up has ensured that the slower pupils have benefitted from the expertise of their quicker fellow pupils; there has been time to hone the paths of recall in the brain, perhaps not to perfection immediately but with improved learning skills and greater accuracy for sure.

[Re. ABC card sets: A statistical analysis of the recurrence of vowels and consonants in various languages would give very different results. German needs many more 'u's than French for example, whereas French will need extra 'e's. If you can get hold of a target language Scrabble board, you will be able to best gauge the proportion of vowels and consonants needed for any particular language. If at a loss, contact a friend in the country and ask them to check for you! Always have a few extra blank cards with the ABC so that letters can be added if necessary.]

All this is good practice and can become part of the daily warm-ups, following the listening exercises, etc. But the best test of recall is just to use the language and, if they have learnt it, they will understand. If they really know it and can recall and produce, then they will use it.

Go to the textbook and see how much they understand. Do some more practice and take them back to the same passage in the textbook. How much more can they understand?

Let them watch a video for a second or third time. Does it make more sense now?

By just looking at a piece of text on one occasion gives pupils no indication of improvement. It is a mere matter of how much do they or don't they understand. By going back to the same piece, after further learning and practice, pupils are given a clear yardstick by which to measure their own progress. The space in between may be as little as a week or as much as a term or even a year; but by re-presenting material to pupils who will, without a shadow of doubt, be able to understand more of it than before, you will be implicity indicating that language learning is not an instant 10/10 or 0/10 subject, but one that grows and grows and builds on everything that has gone before.

The more they see the same words, whether in the same or different contexts, the more their brains will be asked to recognise and recall them. The more often they are asked to do this, the stronger the paths of cognitive procedure required for that recall will be.

If we touch upon something, mention it once or twice and then do not re-visit it for some time, it is not to be wondered at if in the meantime the tenuous structures created in our pupils' brain for both storage and recall will have broken down and the only response we will get from them is a row of blank faces.

# 5.    Language awareness

One of the most misunderstood words in the English language has to be the word 'grammar'. This is not the place to discuss the many meanings that the word has accumulated over the years; all that is needed here is to make clear the sense in which it is meant in this particular context.

For my money, no-one has defined the word as well as Fredrich Bodmer in his *Loom of language* when he said:

> *Having lists of words you know the usual meaning of, will not get you very far (in a language) unless you have knowledge of another kind.*
>
> (Bodmer, 1944;1987)

It is a very apt definition because it illuminates immediately the gap between the expectations of the average Year 7 pupil and reality. If asked what they expect to have to do in order to learn a second language, nearly all of them will reply: 'Learn words'. It is rare that any one of them mentions '. . . and how to string them together to make sense.'

And yet that is precisely what should be occupying their thoughts at least 50% of the time. Of course they do need to learn words — between ten and fifteen a week as already mentioned. But without that other knowledge, of what to do with the words, how to arrange them, in which order to use them to express this idea and which one for that idea, then all they will be left with is a list of words and a handful of phrases learnt off by heart.

The fashion in the 70s and 80s for teaching 'without grammar' did not mean what it said. Grammar cannot be avoided unless you **are** just teaching lists of words. What was meant was 'without explicit grammar'. As the teaching of English grammar waned and the terminology to describe parts of language became as foreign as anything taught as a second language, so pupils understood less and less what they found in the coursebooks. As the teaching of foreign languages themselves spread and overflowed from the academic borders that had held it in a strictly explicit grammatical straitjacket for years, teachers realised that they had a stark choice. Either they taught the grammar from scratch and explained language as language before they moved into the foreign language, or they could adopt different methods in which the grammar patterns could be absorbed implicitly through repetition and use — just as children do with their own mother tongue.

And here we are back at the 'natural learning' theory. I do not deny that repetition and use can and do give learners a feel for grammatical structure and usage — under ideal conditions — which are immersion and intensive courses. These are proven facts. But unfortunately we do not teach in ideal conditions: we may have contact with our pupils for as little as 50 minutes twice a week — which can deliver neither an immersion or an intensive course. Two lessons a week cannot hope to imitate 'natural conditions'.

Rather than spend time investigating the pros and cons of explicit and implicit grammar teaching, let us instead turn the concept round and ask : do we have any evidence that pupils need to know more about

language terminology**?**    the nature of their    the nature of
                            their own language**?**    the target language**?**

As in the previous chapters we shall be looking at the evidence as revealed by the pupils themselves both in their work and their comments. Do we in fact have any evidence that a lack of knowledge of these three things can or does hinder a pupil's progress. Can we predict that without our intervention, they will fall into certain traps.

 ## BUT I LOOKED IT UP IN A DICTIONARY!

Every single language teacher must have a store of these wonderful gaffes. They are the bright sparks that illuminate

> **Je bidon faire ça**
> **Bushaltestelle das! sagt Mutti**

the boredom of marking . . . if one can see them for what they are and that sometimes takes some working out!

Dictionaries are such useful things — unless you don't know the first thing about language and then they are suddenly transformed into linguistic traps. They are more likely to be the source of errors than correct information.

The pupil who wrote the French example looked up the English word he didn't know in a dictionary and there he saw:

> can: (n) bidon (m)
> pot (m): vb pouvoir
> (irreg)

He knew enough to ignore all the information in brackets,

because 'there's no point in looking at it. I don't know what it means.' He then wrote down the French word as given — *bidon. Je bidon faire ça* = I can do that.

The same thing happened to the German student.

She looked up the word she didn't know and found:

> stop: (n) Bushaltestelle
> (f): (vb) auf/hören (vb
> reg. sep.)

It was now a straightforward matter of writing '*Bushaltestelle das! sagt Mutti*'. What could be wrong?

Well, what is wrong is a lack of understanding of what (n) and (vb) mean when met in a dictionary, of what the difference is between their usage and of the difficulties posed by the unique characteristics of the English language.

## UNDERSTANDING ENGLISH FIRST

English unlike other European languages cannot claim to be either a Germanic or Romance language. It is both simultaneously and yet, at the same time, it is neither. Both German and French, the two most widely taught foreign languages in our schools, rely on inflection, gender and agreement, German adhering more strictly to its Indo-European inheritance than French which has managed to rid itself of cases, while keeping strictly to gender and number agreement.

A mish-mash of languages created the English language — Norman French, Anglo-Saxon, Viking, Danish, Celtic — and in doing so some of the patterns from one or other language were retained: we use the German system for verbs, for example, *singen, sang, gesungen* but the French system for emphatic pronouns: 'It's me' not 'I am it'.

Occasionally we retained both. English uniquely has two forms of the comparative and superlative: the German 'big, bigger, the biggest' and the French 'beautiful, more beautiful and the most beautiful'.

But in many instances the conflicting patterns were thrown out and we were left with invariable forms. In the process many of those useful indicators that differentiated between the same idea being used for different functions, such as verb or a noun, an adjective or an adverb, were lost. We have retained some that make clear whether we are dealing with an adjective, for example 'large' 'hungry', rather than the adverb 'largely' 'hungrily'; but we have lost many others or they have become confused. Is 'lovely' an adverb or an adjective? What is the connection between 'good' and 'well'? Between verbs and nouns there can be a difference: 'to write' but 'the writing'; one can't say 'the write' but it is difficult to find these examples. It is far easier to find the opposite: examples of where there is no difference in spelling or form between the verb and the noun, one just uses 'the' in front of the one and 'to' in front of the other — the watch/to watch: the air/to air.

As a result English more than any other European language contains a plethora of homographs — wind (that blows) and wind (a watch) : row (a boat) but row (with your parents): homonyms — bar (to drink in) and bar (when you are no longer allowed in) : fly (the insect) and fly (the plane) and homophones — sew, sow, so; rode, rowed, road; horse, hoarse. The latter caused one student, whose ability in English spelling must have been shaky, to confidently reply to a picture question ' *Worauf reitet sie?*' '*Sie reitet auf einer Heiser*' (She is riding on a hoarse)!

If English pupils are not schooled in the characteristics of their own language before they come into their first foreign language lesson, how are they to be expected to deal with such inconsistencies in their own language. If they are not anticipating that similar spellings can have different meanings or functions, or that similar sounds can be spelt either the same or differently and have totally different meanings and functions, what sense can they be making of the English language? Consider this series of words: bough of a tree, bow of a ship, (homophone) bow of a ship, bow before the Queen (homonym), bow before the Queen, bow and arrows (homograph) bow and arrows, bow in your hair (homonym) bow in your hair, violin bow (homonym) violin bow, wood that bows (homonym).

In a foreign language these would either be totally different words or they would be etymologically related but with different forms. In English they are reduced to two sounds and two spellings for seven meanings, five of which are nouns, two of which are verbs. How can pupils who have not been made explicitly aware of this characteristic of the English language know which word to pick from those offered by a bi-lingual dictionary?

C<small>i</small>LT

It is not as if it would be boring and dull to be given such an insight into English. After all, British comedy relies for much of its humour on such word play. What fun could be had by primary school pupils if asked to make up sentences such as these . . . and then illustrate them.

The farmer sewed the fields          The wind (*wynd) blue a cross the see

To children such sentences appear as fun and nonsense. But an essential lesson **is** being learnt about the nature of the English language: namely, how important it is to thoroughly know any word — its meaning or meanings, its sound or sounds, its spelling or spellings . . . and its function or functions. Without this kind of knowledge, no useful purpose can be served by referring to a dictionary, an activity which is now an integral part of the national MFL curriculum.

 ## PLANNING A COHERENT WHOLE-SCHOOL APPROACH

So, our first step should be to share the burden. We need to talk this through with the English department. We need to know the following:

- Will the children have covered this kind of work by Year 7?
- Will they be continuing it over KS 3?
- Are they to be introduced to dictionary skills?
- When can a pupil be expected to understand, for example, the difference between round (prep) round (n) and round (vb reg)?

> **!** *L*iaise with your colleagues in the English department.

If these things are not already in place, recommend that the two departments work together to create a complementary scheme of work to ensure that, by the end of KS 3, pupils do understand common terminology, can refer with understanding to dictionaries and can make reasoned selections.

So much of what we need to do is mirrored in the demands of the English NC that it is only logical that we should be working together on a homogeneous package aimed at complementing each other's teaching.

 ## NOUNS VS VERBS

In order to make clear the difference between a noun and a verb, I ask Year 7 pupils to cast an eye round the classroom and work out which nouns in the room can very easily become verbs and which nouns cannot. For example: the table — to table ( a motion at a meeting); the chair — to chair (a meeting); the book — to book (a room); the pen — to pen (someone a note) but the window cannot be re-used as a verb. One can't window. To some children this kind of language 'game' comes as a revelation. By themselves they would have never have noticed that they were able to do this in their own language.

The surprise and dawning comprehension is continued when we take a look in our foreign language dictionaries to see how to tell the difference between 'the table/to table', 'the floor/to floor' 'the bag/to bag'. In German the repetitive -*en* verb ending soon becomes clear. In French you can soon start building up columns or groups of verbs with the same endings. For most pupils it will come as a complete surprise that two similar looking words in English have to be translated by two such different looking words in another language.

| the chair | *der Stuhl* | to be in the chair (at a meeting) | *den Vorsitz führen* |
| | *la chaise* | | *présider* |
| the table | *der Tisch* | to table a motion | *einen Antrag einbringen* |
| | *la table* | | *déposer un projet* |

## ANTICIPATE ERRORS

> **!** *K*eep an eye out for possible misunderstandings.

Meet them head-on and pre-empt mistakes by constantly raising pupils' awareness of double entendre or different function or whatever. If the word '(football) match' is going to be used in the next topic, then have the pupils locate the word 'match' in the class dictionaries. Ask them how many different functions it has; how many different nouns is it attached to; do any of the target language translations look like each other?

You can end up with a blackboard looking like this:

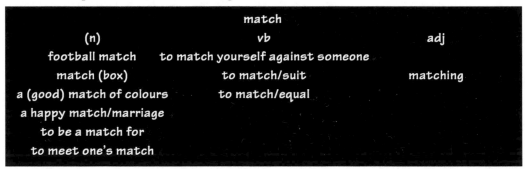

| | match | |
| --- | --- | --- |
| **(n)** | **vb** | **adj** |
| football match | to match yourself against someone | |
| match (box) | to match/suit | matching |
| a (good) match of colours | to match/equal | |
| a happy match/marriage | | |
| to be a match for | | |
| to meet one's match | | |

The principle is the same as before. If we take the time in the early years to make our pupils aware of possible pitfalls, we help them learn to avoid them. Then, as the practice of checking or looking up words becomes part of class routine, so they will need us less and less to emphasise the dangers. They will learn to see them for themselves.

Don't be surprised if your pupils still produce a few howlers! You may well come across misconceptions that you never dreamt of. Luckily all pupils' mistakes can be used by turning them round into exercises. A German friend whose pupils corresponded with mine, sent this extract back to me. It had taken her some time to work out what the writer's intention had been. I should add that we had spent a week in class learning and practising likes and dislikes before the letter was sent!

*'Ich wie zu Schauspiel mein Rekord Spieler'*

A clear case of a pupil going home and not referring to what she had been learning, making no connection between what she wanted to say and what she had been taught. Instead she turned to a dictionary — and used it badly. She was also still at the stage of believing in the transliteration principle of one word in English: one word in German.

However well they may be copying and imitating and seemingly making use of new structures and words in class under our guidance, left to themselves they seem to slide back 'down the snake.' It goes without saying that my next lesson began with a whole class exercise of looking up the word 'like' in the dictionary and finding out what the difference between a (vb) and an (adv) is and then referring back to the page in the coursebook we had just covered!

(Explanation: 'Ich = I; wie = like, as (adv); zu = to (redundant here in German); Schauspiel = play, piece of theatre (noun); mein = my; Rekord = record, best time; Spieler = player.)

## CONSTANT PRACTICE

Dictionary work can easily become one of the regular warm-ups at the beginning of lessons. If the focus of the exercise has immediate relevance and can be put into practice instantly, then all the better. The exercises can be explicit or implicit depending on how you wish to tackle these matters.

Exercises can be very simple

|  | m ou f? | le, la ou l'? | un ou une | mon ou ma? |
|---|---|---|---|---|
| appartement |  |  |  |  |
| maison |  |  |  |  |
| gîte |  |  |  |  |

|  | noun? substantif? | adjective? adjectif? | verb? verbe? | adverb? adverbe? |
|---|---|---|---|---|
| flat |  |  |  |  |
| house |  |  |  |  |
| garden |  |  |  |  |
| well |  |  |  |  |
| flower |  |  |  |  |

or can require much more investigation and thought.

It is not just a knowledge of morphology and terminology that is needed to make sensible use of a dictionary. Even the simplest of things must be highlighted and explained, if pupils are not to fall into more traps. What, for example, does the following reveal about the understanding of English by the pupil who produced it?

Starting from the back: '*il*' = it. Obviously this pupil has been taught that *il* = he or it. What he or she doesn't understand is the difference between a subject and an object pronoun and because English uses the same word in sentences such as 'It is here' and 'I see it', he or she takes it as read that the target language will do the same.

*Trouvaille:* another example of a pupil making use of much too sophisticated a dictionary. If 'find' 1. (n) *trouvaille* f. was the first entry, this dictionary is not the kind to be recommended to beginners.

And then '*argot*'. I had to search through five different dictionaries before I discovered one that gave '*argot*' as the first translation of the word this pupil was obviously looking up.

If you ignore apostrophes because you don't really have a clue why they are there — and many pupils do ignore what they don't see as relevant — then of course you, too, would look up 'can't' as 'cant' and if you have a certain sort of dictionary, the first word given under 'cant' will be '*argot*'. It could just as easily have been '*langage hypocrite*' or '*cafarderie*' or even '*afféterie*' or even '*jargon*'.

They make a good pair of examples . . .

| | |
|---|---|
| '*Je bidon faire ça*' | '*Je argot trouvaille il*' |
| I can do that | I can't find it |

. . . and illustrate between them so well the need for knowledge of language — written in the National Curriculum with capital letters: Knowledge of Language (KoL). It is essential that our pupils have an understanding of the different functions of words, the relevance of spelling and multiple meaning, of abbreviation and ellision. The examples above reveal some of the pitfalls our unsuspecting pupils may fall into when they try to produce new language by themselves. They provide evidence to support Ringbom's theory already quoted: that beginners will expect the target language to behave as their own with just lexical items being different.

 ## STRUCTURES ARE IMPORTANT TOO

If this theory is sustainable, we should be able to predict this kind of behaviour — transliteration — in our pupils. In addition, we should expect them to fall into linguistic traps — more or less on a sliding scale depending on how much direct and explicit teaching of language they have received, before beginning their first foreign language.

How are we to help our pupils avoid transliteration or at least — if transliteration is a natural step in foreign language learning — how do we accelerate their progress through this stage so that they come out quickly on the other side with the lesson well learnt?

Once again Fredrich Bodmer shows the way. As long ago as 1944 he was advocating the triple translation technique; the target language, the transliteration, the English.

*Je les ai vues à l'école*
I them have seen to the school
*I saw them at school*

*Ich habe sie in der Schule gesehen*
I have them in the school seen
*I saw them at school*

I have always used this system myself in the belief that if pupils understand the value of each separate unit of a phrase, they can quickly learn to transfer these elements to create new but similar structures. It also has the benefit of using transliteration but clearly not stopping there. If pupils are naturally going to treat the foreign language in the same way as their own, with only a change of words, then we need to take this misconception and move it very deliberately and positively one step further to arrive at the right solution.

So, from the beginning phrases such as *Je m'appelle* are introduced as meaning 'I myself call' and the English meaning is given as either 'I'm . . .' or 'My name is . . .' or 'I'm called . . .'

The implicit lesson being learnt here is twofold: one — that the French and English structures are different and: two — English often offers a variety of phrases, all of which equally well address one single target language idea or concept.

This is yet another important message to get across:  ⟶

> **!** *U*se is more important than looks: function before form.

Our pupils are not required to analyse the **function** of the words and structures they use in English. As a result they are totally unaware, for example, that 'bigger' and 'more beautiful ' share the same function — that they are both comparative forms. Because the two forms look different, pupils do not expect them to have any connection and so it will not occur to them to look for it. They will also expect to translate them differently into the target language. Similarly, they find it hard to grasp that four different ways of saying walk — I walk, I do walk, I am walking and I have been walking — can all be equally valid ways of indicating the Present Tense of a verb.

In the target language they have to understand that same concepts are realised by same forms: so bigger and more beautiful will have the same construction: *'plus grand'*, *'plus beau'* — *'größer'*, *'schöner'*. At some stage, they have to discover for themselves, or have revealed to them, that all four forms of any English Present Tense serve one function and so will be translated by a single form in the target language: *je vais, ich gehe*.

The three-stage or triple translation technique can direct their attention to many grammatical features: cases, word order, idiom, the frequency of similiarities and dissimilarities between the mother tongue and the target language. And it is not a system the pupils find at all difficult. In class I have often overheard pupils working in a group recall using the triple translation and so avoid staying put at the transliteration stage.

> **!** *P*upils have to be helped to look beyond form to function.

'*Le grand chien noir* . . . what's that? the . . . big . . . dog . . . black . . . Ah ha . . . The big black dog.'

'Doesn't 'go' have to go to the end? I must today in the town go. That's what it has to be.'

*'Il me la donne samedi matin* . . . Hum? He . . . me . . . the . . . meaning it . . . from a *'la '* word
. . . gives . . . Saturday morning. Hummm . . . He gives me it on Saturday morning? . . . What
about: He'll give me it on Saturday morning . . . that makes more sense here.'

It is at moments like this when what you have taught comes boomeranging back via their
memories and recall, and you know you have given them vital 'tags' in their recall system, 'tags'
that stimulate the processes of locating internal information and then internal checking. By
deliberately using transliteration as an intermediate stage, we train them not to expect it to be the
final stage. By translating one word for one word, pupils can hear and see for themselves the false
English that that process creates. Their common sense and their feeling for their own language
will prompt them to offer other suggestions and in the process they become aware that, as in the
example above, a French Present Tense may be used to convey something we might use a Future
Tense for.

This common sense and feel for language is evident in what the pupils say as they play around
with words out loud. But it can also appear as a silent reaction. If I see children write something
and then look silently at it, I congratulate them. 'What for?' they ask.' I haven't done anything.
I was just looking at what I'd written.' 'Precisely!' I tell them. 'Well done! Giving your brain a
chance to check it . . . excellent!'

What I hope, what I am sure, is going on inside, is an internal aural or visual check.


## DEVELOPING A FEEL FOR LANGUAGE

The importance of training pupils to check their work by re-reading has already been highlighted.
One of my favourite ways of encouraging and developing this internal checking is, once again,
by the use of a computer program. The second in the series of three mentioned earlier, this one
practises structure: Word Sequencing or *Pêle-Mêle/Satzspiel* was originally designed for the
TEFL market, but its potential for modern languages was immediately apparent.

A very simple program, it can offer pupils some of the most important practice over the initial
learning period when new concepts are being built, when new cognitive procedures are being
developed or when existing procedures are being added to or adapted.

It is a word jumbler. That's all. It means you can enter sentences ranging from

*Je m' appelle Jean*                    *Ich wohne in der Nähe von Birmingham*
to
*Il ne me les a pas données*            *Ich habe es ihm letzte Woche geschenkt*

and the computer will jumble them randomly into something like this:

*m' Jean Je appelle*                    *Nähe von wohne in Ich Birmingham der*
*les données Il pas ne a me*            *es letzte habe Woche geschenkt Ich ihm*

There are only two ways in which one is able to sort out the right answer. By checking with a correct image seen inside your head or by checking against a correct version heard inside your head. And it is, strangely enough, the latter that most pupils use. When asked how they have arrived at their solution and what makes them think that it is correct, the usual reply is 'It sounds right'. When it is pointed out to them that neither they nor the computer have said anything, so how can it sound right, they tap their heads and say 'It sounds right in here'.

The contents of the files comprise all the latest structures they have met in class. It would make no sense to sort out sentences they haven't heard or seen. During the first and, may be, subsequent goes, I give aural backup by calling out the sentences as the pupils are working through the computer exercise . This has the added advantage that where, in a language like French, the sound differs from the sight of words and phrases, pupils can match sound and individual elements and so build up an internal vision and attach sound to it. It also means that they are holding the sound and cadence of the sentence in short-term memory.

At first pupils find the unjumbling difficult, but as they practise and practise the same exercise, they become ever more accurate and fast.

Listed below are the times of a pupil working in the first term of Year 7, practising not only matching genders by locating the correct article to noun but also adding the correct form of the adjective to the nouns.

| sentence | date 7 Nov 1st attempt | 2nd attempt | 14 Nov 3rd attempt | 21 Nov 4th attempt | 5th attempt |
|---|---|---|---|---|---|
| Un crayon rouge et des ciseaux rouges | 2m08 | 32 secs | 1m51 | 14 secs | 31 secs * |
| Une règle verte et un crayon vert | 2m18 | 42 secs | 24 secs | 19 secs | 17 secs |
| Des cahiers jaunes et un livre jaune | | 48 secs | 2m12 ** | | 17 secs |

**Explanation:**
* the video shows that the group was distracted by other pupils during this particular answering sequence. The 31 secs should not be seen as definitive; the average that lesson was 24 and 26 seconds
** This marks the beginning of an interesting muddle when one member of the group suddenly insisted on placing the adjectives in the English way. see below

No entry indicates that that particular sentence did not appear at that attempt.

The jumbles may have looked like this:

*rouges rouge et des Un crayon crayons*
*et un vert règle verte Une crayon*
*jaune cahiers un jaunes livre et Des*

The most obvious conclusion to be drawn even from these few results is that from one end of November to the other, the pupil became much more adept at recognising what word went with what word. English eyes and brains do not have to look at ends of words to find gender or number agreements. But it is impossible to do this exercise without doing just that. Within three weeks, after three 25-minute sessions, her eyes and her attention had been focused on looking for '*s*' plurals or '*une*' + '*e*' on the adjective as opposed to no agreement.

To be able to recognise what the correct answer should be and actually physically sort it out in seventeen seconds is skilled and pupil confidence soars. That the exercise is laying down good recognition patterns, good internal checking with correctly stored patterns of language, is what I believe gives this program its value. And, perhaps even more importantly, it offers rapid enough repetition to highlight and then eliminate errors, such as the muddle that occurred in the second week.

Although on 7 November the pupil had been slow to reach accuracy, she did improve quite remarkably over the session, eventually recording a final time of 42" for the last sentence compared to a time of 2'08" for the first.

Then on 14 November something unaccountable occurred after the first three sentences had been sorted in times of 1'51", 24" and 48" respectively. She suddenly placed the adjectives in front of the nouns, i.e. used English word order. It took 2'54" to work out what was wrong and then only because she overheard what I was saying to someone else. The next sentence passes off well and then the same thing occurred with sentence no. 5 . . . adjectives in the English position. She can be heard trying out the gender of the nouns '*Une calculette? Une compas?*' before moving the words. She then moved the nouns back again and at last moved the adjectives. The sigh of relief as the computer congratulates her success is audible!

At the second attempt, sentences 1 and 2 posed no problems but then with the next four sentences she insisted on placing the adjectives in the wrong place again. Having been told by the computer that this was wrong, she tried out various strategies — swapping the nouns, swapping the adjectives, staring at the screen. On sentences no. 3 and 6 she called to a neighbour for help. On the latter occasion he started to say '*Une calculette . . .*' and she interrupted ' . . . *et un sac blue* (sic)'. She then correctly sorts the sentence. These four sentences have taken her: 2'09", 2'12", 1'19" and 1'11".

She ended the lesson with a third attempt at the exercise. She correctly sorted the first sentence: *Un stylo vert et des livres verts*. But the second sentence was given English style adjectives again. '*Un blanc sac et des blancs feutres*' and of course she was told she was wrong. She stared at the screen for twenty seconds and then called me over. I suggested she read it aloud, which she did. She immediately made the correction but then paused and stared at the screen for 21 seconds. Was she checking to see whether she was right? Was she reading it silently to herself? What ever was happening in her brain, she pressed the key to check her answer and was of course rewarded for her effort. The next three sentences are then all re-sorted accuractely and without hesitation.

During the third lesson spent on this same exercise the following week, this pupil recorded average times of 24 and 26 seconds. In her last attempt eight out of nine sentences were sorted, not merely correctly, but without a single incorrect movement of any word. She went for the right order straight away.

Something important happened here. Learning had gone on.

And what is more, we can follow the pupil's progress as she begins to make sense of what to her brain is, at the beginning, linguistic nonsense. The new concepts being dealt with here have no counterparts in English: noun genders and adjective agreements. As she moves from random action via application of various strategies to correct procedures and thought processes, we can watch various behaviours — some not altogether unexpected.

- Initially we have evidence of random sorting.
- We have evidence of mother tongue influence and its comparatively speedy eradication.
- We have, on one occasion, possible evidence that transliteration is being used as a reminder '*Un sac blue*'(sic).
- We have definite evidence for the usefulness of reading solutions aloud as a check.
- The video also reveals murmuring during pauses, which I take to be a half way house between sounding out loud and sounding out internally, especially as they are usually followed by correct or corrected solutions.

It is a truism to say that one does not do what one can't do. Similarly, one does do what one can do. But in the reality and context of school work, these truisms are often ignored or changed. Instead they are erroneously understood as:

- one cannot do what one hasn't bothered to spend time learning;
- one cannot do what is too difficult for one to do;
- one cannot do what one is not putting enough effort in to try and do.

With foreign language learning truisms prevail. Pupils cannot be expected just to take a new concept on board one moment and apply it correctly in all circumstances from that time on. When pupils have had sufficient opportunity to overcome all the natural tendencies and influences of their own language, then they may be able to apply the new concept correctly. To ask for accurate performance from them before this is established, is to ask for failure. Not to give opportunities to be able to overcome, suppress or by-pass existing automatic cognitive influences is to delay this whole process of learning a second language. If these opportunities can be in close succession, with instant correction, then random efforts can become systematised, influences can be corrected and minimised and the correct procedures for resolution can become well-trodden paths of cognitive behaviour.

It is precisely these opportunities that a computer can offer. I wonder how many practice lessons in the classroom and how many written exercises in an exercise book would have had to have been done over what kind of period of time to have achieved the same amount of learning, as achieved in those three 25-minute lessons?

# 6. The concept of grammar

It is a strange fact that the further back in time you trace the European languages, the more strictly grammatical patterns apply. Our ancestors 2,000 or 20,000 years ago would not have tolerated such 'sloppiness' in their language as the homonyms and homophones listed earlier. Nor would they have been happy with invariable forms to serve different functions. To them a noun had to sound like a noun and had somehow to indicate clearly whether it was the subject of a sentence or the object or the indirect object or being used prepositionally. An adjective had to show clearly which noun it was attached to; it could never have been mistaken for an adverb. But then in those days they did not have strict rules about word order. If words can be put in any order, then so many of the characteristics of the languages our ancestors developed for themselves make sense.

A number of words strung one after the other with no apparent connection cannot be understood. Context might on reflection give the meaning, but language has to work faster than that. There might not be time to think.

> small big cave bear black dark in lives

Which cave? The small one or the big one? The black one or the dark one? And is it the cave that is big? Or the bear?

But if the words have some pattern to them that clearly links them, whatever their position, at least their relationship is clearer.

> caveX dark Y blackX bearY bigY inX smallX livesY

English relies almost entirely on linear word order and proximity to make relationships clear.

> The big dark bear lives in the small black cave.

No-one ever sat down and dictated the grammar of a language. It evolved with the people, satisfying their particular needs for communication and the way in which they wished to express themselves.

## THE PERSPECTIVE OF THOUGHT

It is not just a case of sounding different — which of course different languages do do — but a matter of thinking differently. The thinking is different because each language lays greater or lesser importance on different salient features in the ideas its people are trying to communicate. I call these perspectives of thought and from them come the grammatical differences which shape individual languages.

The universality of language is what unites all human beings across the globe. The different perspectives of thought is what differentiates our languages.

CiLT

Look at this picture.

When the French wish to convey this thought, they have to say:

*Jean donne l'argent à l'homme.*

where the four separate images that comprise this idea i) John the giver ii) the act of giving iii) what is being given and iv) the person to whom it is being given are seen in that order.

The Germans, however, would see it differently:

*Johann gibt dem Mann das Geld.*

For the Germans the perspective changes and our mind having first taken in John as the giver (i), secondly the act of giving (ii), then sees the person to whom it is being given as the next important piece of information (iv); what is being given comes last (iii). The images that comprise the idea are being seen in a different order from the French.

Because English has both these languages as parents, it should come as no surprise that we can say it either way. We have in this instance decided to keep both perspectives, so we can say

|  | John gives the money to Robert | French perspective |
|---|---|---|
| or | John gives Robert the money | German perspective |

If we wished to communicate the same idea but using pronouns instead, the perspectives change quite dramatically.

The French now see i) the giver, then iii) the object given, then iv) the person to whom it is given and finally ii) the act of giving. Is it the pronouns that have moved? Or the verb?

*Jean le lui donne.*

The Germans also change the order. Now they prefer placing the object given before the person to whom it is being given. To do this they have to reverse the previous order.

*Johann gibt dem Mann das Geld.*          *Johann gibt es ihm.*

And the English? Well the English say — why bother changing a couple of good perspectives! It makes no changes at all and retains the noun word order exactly.

John gives the money to the man          John gives the man the money
John gives it to him                     John gives him it.

Grammar, as understood by the grammar found in textbooks or grammar books, is in the main a way of codifying in words and examples all these perspectives. In order to learn another language, we need to understand its perspectives of thought and the characteristics of the individual images that comprise those thoughts. We can very often understand these best by 'seeing' the concept at work in our mind's eye, by imagining the whole idea as a series of individual images and noting how and when their perspective or an individual characteristic differs from ours. Once we can do this, we have a language's grammar.

It will help if we can put ourselves 'in the linguistic shoes' of the target language and find, not only differences between their perspectives and ours, but perhaps also even reasons for them.

## THE LOGIC OF FRENCH ADJECTIVES

When introducing French adjectives, I tell the pupils that, except for a limited number, all adjectives will follow the noun. That the French say 'a house white, my bike green, my small dog black, etc'. Someone in the class usually makes the comment 'how silly' or words to that effect. I immediately pick up this comment and turn it back to the class. 'Is it silly? Listen carefully, because what I am going to say is very, very important. At the end of this lesson I am going to give each and every one of you a red . . . soft . . . furry . . . round . . . Uhhhhhhh!' and I collapse dramatically across the table without finishing the sentence!

'What am I going to give you?' I ask on immediately resurrecting myself.

'Something furry', 'A round red thing something', 'It was soft and furry' come the answers. 'You didn't get round to saying!' someone will remark.

'And that was English adjective word order, adjectives in a string and then at the end the noun, the item being described. Now listen again but this time I'll use the French system. At the end of this lesson I am going to give each and every one of you a cushion, soft, furry, round, red. You probably don't want it . . . but at least you know this time what you're getting. Which way is clearer? And why?'

What follows is a simple straightforward language activity and discussion. By the end of it, the pupils will be freely admitting that the French is a better system. That you can't begin to picture the English idea until you get to the noun or item. As they were listening, they were all seeing different objects in their minds eye. Whereas with the French system, if you say the item first and then describe it, you can follow very easily in the mind's eye, changing the image as the adjectives are heard.

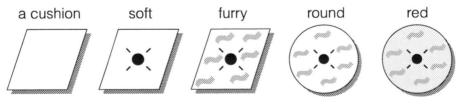

This kind of reasoning can work just as well with concepts that do not even occur in our language. So you can introduce new concepts as well as re-order existing ones and ask pupils to judge them.

## The accuracy of case endings

In order to introduce the concept of cases in German, I play on their usefulness. On the board I draw three pots sherds, one of which has 'the man' written on it, another 'the dog' and the third one 'bit'. And I ask the class to imagine that they are archaeologists who have discovered these three bits which obviously come from the same piece of pottery. 'What was the original sentence?'

The immediate response is 'The dog bit the man', though the chief joker in the class very often offers 'The man bit the dog'. If this happens, I nod and congratulate him or her — to their surprise — and point out that probability is not the same thing as possibility. Both sentences are possible. Only one is probable.

I then draw three more sherds.
On these are written
*Der Mann, den Hund* and *biß*.

This time they have to be German archaeologists, but before they make up their minds they have to know that '*der*' indicates the person/thing doing the action and '*den*' the person or thing it is being done to. 'Now what was the original sentence?'

And of course there is only one solution. 'The man bit the dog.'

'What would you have to say for it to mean the other way round?'
'*Der . . . Hund biß . . . den . . . Mann.*'
'Correct! And which is the more reliable system? Which is the clearer? Which is unequivocal, i.e. can't be mistaken for anything else, has only one meaning?'

By offering reasons and simple demonstrations which all can understand, the obstacle of learning a new concept is reduced, if not removed. The learning to apply will still take time, but the bafflement caused by coming across a new concept is minimised.

Because we all share the ability to think in ideas and images, thought pictures and their perspectives can be one way of approaching the larger grammatical dimension. Having understood the concept, however, there is still the realisation of each individual image into foreign words and this can sometimes call for new procedures of storage and recall.

## Dealing with gender

We cannot, for example, use any existing English procedures to store or recall the definite articles in French because we have never been asked by our language to do such a thing. There is nothing in our grammar system that requires us to store four different words like '*le*', '*la*', '*l'*' and '*les*' from which we have to choose one.

We do have a system for choosing between two — this and these: that and those. So choice between singular and plural is already something we recognise. We also have a system for changing a word if the following word begins with a vowel: a pear but an apple. So checking for nouns with initial vowels is not unknown to us. So why not make use of these existing systems to create a new one to cope with the French?

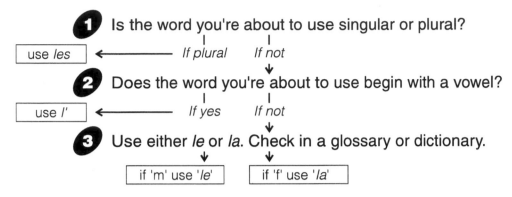

**1** Is the word you're about to use singular or plural?

use *les* ← If plural    If not

**2** Does the word you're about to use begin with a vowel?

use *l'* ← If yes    If not

**3** Use either *le* or *la*. Check in a glossary or dictionary.

if 'm' use '*le*'    if 'f' use '*la*'

This is a procedure that can become part and parcel of routine classwork during the early learning period. If it is repeated often enough as a conscious procedure, it will eventually become an internal process, which will then become automatic routine. The brain will have been given a definite route of thought to follow in order to retrieve the information required. Pupils often balk at step 3 — 'It's such a fiddle!' 'I can't be bothered'. But they should be encouraged by being told that it doesn't last for ever, that when they have looked up the same word three times and each time have anticipated the correct gender, then they have got to the point when they no longer need to check that word.

### PRACTISING GENDERS

The idea of using a dictionary to check gender can be used to create an exercise for pairwork.

* Each pupil writes down any six words from the current topic with what they believe to be the correct gender.
* The list is then passed to the other person for checking.
* First of all that person ticks the words they believe to be right and crosses the words they think have been given the wrong gender.
* Then they check in a dictionary / glossary and in the second column tick or cross whether the original entry was correct or not.

There will be two results: pupil 1 may have got 5/6 right and pupil 2 may have spotted the mistake and so gets 6/6.

The marker's score is calculated by the number of matching X's and ✓'s in the two columns.

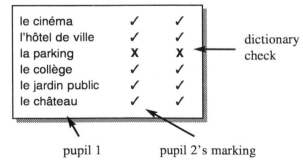

| | pupil 1 | pupil 2's marking | |
|---|---|---|---|
| le cinéma | ✓ | ✓ | |
| l'hôtel de ville | ✓ | ✓ | dictionary |
| la parking | X | X | check |
| le collège | ✓ | ✓ | |
| le jardin public | ✓ | ✓ | |
| le château | ✓ | ✓ | |

**CiLT**

Pupil 2 may have got 4/6 right and pupil 1 may have considered two of those wrong, when in fact they were right and did not spot either of the other two, leaving him or her with a score of just 2/6.

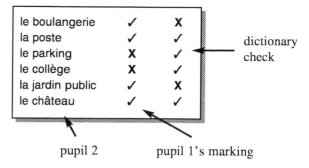

| le boulangerie | ✓ | X |
| la poste | ✓ | ✓ |
| le parking | X | ✓ |
| le collège | X | ✓ |
| la jardin public | ✓ | X |
| le château | ✓ | ✓ |

dictionary check

pupil 2          pupil 1's marking

There are only two matching symbols in the two columns, so pupil 1 scores only two points, whereas four of the original entries were correct, so pupil 2 gets 4/6.

Another exercise for pairs: it needs no preparation and so can be used impromptu.

- Each of the two pupils writes a list of six to eight words learnt recently. The list could be in English or just give the target language noun.
- They then swap lists and have to add the correct gender or gender and TL word for each word on the other's list.
- The trick is that each pupil must be able to correct the other's effort, i.e. has got to know the answer themselves . . . or check if there is any dispute.

The articles to be added do not have to be the definite article: as they are learnt, a point could be made of adding indefinites, possessives, demonstratives.

## STORING GENDER

Research done in Canada by André Rigault revealed that the French appear to retrieve gender aurally, that the pattern of sound made by a word suggests which gender it is likely to be.

To encourage and develop similar skills, brief listening exercises could be included in the warm-ups, in which pupils listen to words and have to write them down in the correct column headed — 'le' or 'la' or 'der', 'die' or 'das'. Most adult grammars give lists of endings which normally fall into one of the two categories. As and when any of these ending patterns apply to vocabulary being learnt, they could be emphasised. In French, for example, there are some very clear differences where people or animals are involved and it would be encouraging always to include at least some of these: *fermier/fermière; acteur/actrice; marchand/marchande; chat/chatte.* In German the connections between spelling and gender are even clearer and should be similarly passed on as tips little by little as they are encountered.

## SEEING GENDER

Some children are very spatially aware. This awareness can be harnessed to reinforce gender of new vocabulary by allocating one wall of the classroom to pictures/flashcards of masculine words and another to feminine words; obviously, a third wall is required for the neuter in German and the remaining wall can hold plurals. As new words are introduced, they can be pinned up on the appropriate wall. Charts mapping the articles and pronouns for that gender can also by pinned up as a further source of reference. Use of wall charts as prompts is allowed up to Level 4 for Speaking and Level 3 for Writing

The benefits of this system remain with some pupils throughout the five years. 'I always remember that word. It was just over my friend's shoulder . . . on the wall behind her . . . Every time I looked at her, I saw it. I can still see it.' 'To remember whether it's a '*le*' or '*la*' word I just think . . . did I see it up there on the right or the left? If I can 'see' it on the left, then I know it's '*le*'.

 ### ACTIVE LEARNING

V.J. Cook in his essay 'Second Language Learning' concluded:

> *Above all the teacher should recognise the active contribution made by the learner; regardless of what the teacher wants him* (sic) *to do, the learner adopts certain learning and production strategies; success in learning is a product of many different factors in the learner, most of them out of the teacher's control.*
>
> (Cook, 1982)

To bring some of these more under the control of the teacher, I turn to the computer again. In the previous chapters it has been suggested that the computer can make a unique contribution to learning because of its ability to monitor step by step pupils' own thinking, correcting and redirecting wrong thought procedures. I am now going to suggest another area in which the computer can contribute.

The essence of this chapter on the concept of grammar has been the necessity of building up inside the pupils' minds images of new or different concepts and procedures of thought which will either be adaptations of those already existing or totally new paths to be carved in the mind.

We have traditionally given our pupils verbal directions to the paths they have to take and made them learn them off by heart. For example, we have told them that the past participle is made by taking off the -*er* and adding -*é*, -*ir* and adding -*i*, -*re* and adding -*u*, etc; that the order of pronouns is *me, te, se, nous, vous, le, la, les*, etc; that the verb must be in second position, except in a subordinate clause where it will be placed at the end.

CiLT

And for some pupils these verbal directions are enough. They can take them into their brain and, with a bit of practice, apply them for ever more. But for the greater majority, they remain like distant commandments; pupils know they should follow them but, in the hurly burly of reality, forget to do so.

If, however, the verbal direction can be converted into real activity, then the storing and recalling processes of the mind get yet another chance at learning. If we are telling our pupils that the past participle is created by taking off the -er and adding an é, why not let them actually do it . . . on the computer. Using a word processor and its facilities to delete, insert and move, many of the individual grammatical points can be turned into graphic reality.

## ACTIVE GRAMMAR

In this exercise, the computer screen has a 'notepad' created in the middle of the screen. Above and below are the separate components of the perfect tense. The notepad has the English prompts. The pupil highlights the appropriate subject + form of *avoir*, '*j'ai*' and copies it to the notepad by pressing CTRL + C, moving the cursor into the notepad, placing it at the end of the first sentence and pressing CTRL + V. They repeat the copy process for the correct infinitive '*attendre*' and then actively do what the teacher has been describing. They remove the -re and add -u: '*attendre*' >> '*attend-*' >> '*attendu*'.

> j'ai  tu as   il a   elle a
>
> I have waited  j'ai attendu
> she has found  elle a trouv
> he sold
>
> trouver  jouer  chercher  finir
> remplir  choisir  attendre
> perdre  vendre

By turning verbal descriptions into actions, the pupils not only experience the reality of the words, but are also left with a visual image of actually doing what they have been told to do mentally. It is much easier to recall images of actions, than mere words. This is a powerful learning experience, far more so than any written exercise on paper.

We can use and re-use the facilities of word processors to enhance the nuts and bolts of grammar learning throughout the learning period, but it is of greatest use when we are trying to establish and develop both a new concept and its retrieval path.

If we tell pupils that French pronouns come in front of the verb, why not let them do it — for real.

> *Jean mange les frites.*
> Delete the '*frites*'.
> *Jean mange les*
> Highlight the '*les*'
> *Jean mange les*
> Drag the highlighted block in front of '*mange*'
> *Jean les mange*
> *Voilà!*

If we tell our pupils that certain prepositions are always followed by the accusative (or direct object), why don't we let them have a go at doing just that — not on pen and paper where mistakes stay obvious for ever — even after the application of Liquid Paper, but on screen where we can highlight, colour, hide and do all sorts of things to make the information obtainable and the practice enjoyable.

The pupils can play around cutting and pasting or copying and pasting or highlighting and dragging knowing that if they get it wrong, the signs will not be left for all to see. They can have as many goes as they like in private until they get it right! And when they have practised enough, then they can turn public performance into permanence and put it on paper.

---

durch für gegen ohne um entlang

| den | die | das |
| einen | eine | ein |
| meinen | meine | mein |
| | | |
| Baum | Tür | Haus |
| Vater | Wand | Tor |
| Mauer | Mutter | Mädchen |

for my mother         für mein**e**
against the wall
without a girl
through the door

Erfinde noch andere! Deutsch und Englisch bitte!

---

If new ideas are to form in pupils' heads and if practice strengthens the embryonic retrieval lines and reinforces the patterns of thought, we should be allowing our pupils much more time to play around with the words and structures, before we ask them to do anything with them.

We should not consider extended practice a waste of time. We should be taking as much time as the pupils in front of us need. For some it will take a longer, for others a shorter time. But if we do not ensure comprehension of concept, sound learning techniques, adequate time to evolve a good recall system, then we should not be surprised, when the initial fervour of the pupils runs out of steam — somewhere round about Level 4.

Suddenly the next steps along the continuum of learning appear insurmountable — as in truth they are for many. All buildings need foundations; if care is taken to build solid foundations, then the brick walls take no time at all to be erected. But if the walls are built directly onto the ground, then the weight of a few courses of bricks will cause the whole building to sink into the mud.

If our pupils are to get beyond the first few levels of the NC MFL where mere imitation and repetition and a handful of phrases learnt as whole sounds off by heart will suffice, they will need to have a better understanding of language, more time to accustom their eyes and ears to the new language and have to spend more time in preparation before the end result — performing in the target language.

C*i*LT

Rather than us dictating the pace of learning in the early years, we should be ensuring that the individual needs of our pupils are being addressed. If they can't do something, it could be, because:

- we are asking them to do it too soon;
- we have not given them enough time to absorb the new work;
- we have not helped them find an effective way of learning;
- we haven't taken into account their own hypotheses on language and language learning or uncovered any possible misconceptions;
- we haven't asked them where the problem lies.

We cannot rely on our pupils each having a copy of Collins Robert (Standard size) by their side, for example, to pre-empt all their possible misconceptions

Unless we analyse the mistakes they are making, we will not know which particular hurdles they are facing at any one time.

| cant[1] | 1 n (pej) (a) (insincere talk) langage m de convention, phrases toutes faites (b) (jargon) jargon m argot m de métier |
| | 2 vi parler avec hypocrisie ou affectation |
| cant[2] | 1 n (a) (slope, steepness) pente f (b) (jolt) secousse f |
| can't | abbr of cannot; V can |

If we don't probe their learning styles and ask them to share the problems and difficulties they may be having, they may be developing silently all sorts of hypotheses which may in the end prevent any real progress.

And if we make light of the task they are facing, instead of pointing out that this is going to be a long slow haul — but one which they are all capable of in the long run — they may become discouraged at their seeming lack of progress after all the effort they are putting in.

> *One assumption that is widely held as axiomatic is that people learn by doing. We seem to have deduced that people learn to speak by speaking and so on.*
> *In reality one simply drowns by attempting to swim without some sort of prior preparation or theoretical instruction.*
> *Obviously the art of speaking can be improved by practice, but the skill of speaking is learnt primarily in a vast complex of other ways. It might be suggested that listening and reading contribute more to the assimilation of language, certainly at the L2 stage.*
>
> (David Walls, 1992)

One thing we can assure them — anyone can speak a second language . . . or a third or a fourth. It is just that they are not learning it under ideal conditions. That having been said, with only on average two hours of lessons per week over five years, the time spent learning by the average pupil is the equivalent of spending fifteen days in the country concerned. They make a great deal more progress over the five years than they would do if they visited the country for just over a fortnight. So comparatively, for the time spent, their effort really is worthwhile.

# References and further reading

Ackermann D, *A natural history of the senses* (Phoenix/Orion, 1996)

BBC2 Horizon, *The man who made up his mind* (BBC Educational, 1994)

Bernhardt E, *Life in language immersion classrooms* (Multilingual Matters, 1992)

Bernhardt E, 'Cognitive processes in L2: an examination of reading behaviours' in Lantolf and Labarca, *Research in second language learning: focus on the classroom* (New Jersey: Ablex Corp, 1987)

Berwick G and P Horsfall, *Making effective use of the dictionary* (CILT, 1996)

Bodmer F, *The loom of language* (1944; reprinted Merlin, 1987)

Channel 4 & Green Umbrella Ltd and QWGBH Boston, *The mystery of the senses: sight* (1995) (see also Ackermann above)

Cook V J, 'Second language learning: a psycholinguistic perspective' in Kinsella V (ed), *Surveys 1* (CUP, 1982)

DES, *Modern foreign languges for ages 11–16* (1990)

Edelman G, *Neural Darwinism* (Penguin, 1987)

Edelman G, *Bright air, brilliant fire* (Penguin, 1992)

Hawkins E, *Modern languages in the curriculum* (CUP, 1981)

Hewer S, 'Information technology' in Hawkins E (ed), *Thirty years of language teaching* (CILT, 1996)

Manning P, 'Computers, learners and teaching strategies' in *EUROCALL 1991* (Helsinki)

Rigault A, *La grammaire du français parlé* (Hachette, 1971)

Ringbom H, *The role of the first language in the foreign language learning classroom* (Multilingual Matters, 1987)

Ringbom H, 'Cross-linguistic influence and the foreign language learning process' in Kellerman and Sharwood-Smith, *Cross-linguistic influence in second language acquisition* (Pergamon, 1986)

Walls D, 'Survival of fluency?' in *ReCALL 7* (1992)